MAKE MORE MONEY SPEAKING

*For Profit Minded Entrepreneurs &
Executives…Even If You Hate Selling Or Have
Never Spoken On Stage!*

BY GARY LAFFERTY
VERSION 1.3

Free - Bonus Training

This online training contains step-by-step instructions that you can use RIGHT NOW on how you can Turn Every Talk (Big or Small) into a Tidal wave of Profitable Opportunities!

No List or Experience Required.

Get it NOW at

www.MakeMoreMoney-Speaking.com/Masterclass

Endorsements and Accolades

"Gary is bar-none the greatest presenter I have ever met. He is personable and likeable, and translates that into a fantastic sales presence. He is always a professional, and will make the best of difficult situations. He is an asset to any business."

Blakeley Davies, Office and Logistics Manager at Wines by Geoff Hardy, Australia

"Gary is a great speaker who always seizes to get the best possible performance out of his colleagues and people he manages. He is a wonderful motivator with a never-ending positive attitude."

Franziska Kracht, Freelance Journalist for TV, Social and Radio, Germany

"Gary Lafferty – simply phenomenal – an individual who delivers with absolute integrity when presenting on stage in front of large audiences with acute knowledge of various subject matters including business growth. Gary is a natural and has an amazing ability to win over audiences with a charm that is second to none – I have yet to come across someone who is as enthusiastic and energetic as Gary"

Raggi Gandham, Top-performing Recruiter, London, United Kingdom

"Gary's presenting and teaching is superlative, innovative and extremely motivational. Generous in his knowledge sharing and an all round pleasure to work with."

Emmanuel Orelaja, Financial Markets Trader & Mentor - London, United Kingdom

"Gary is a very passionate and enthusiastic speaker. He motivates everyone during his presentations and gives the necessary drive to inspire to take action to achieve your goals."

Viv Oliver, Author, Fast Result and Success Coach, Mentor & Motivational Speaker, London, United Kingdom

"Gary is a world-class presenter. He is extremely passionate about trading and always delivers a first class event. He understands how to teach so people learn quickly and enjoy the process. If you have the chance to work with him or learn from him I would grab it with both hands now!"

Sara Davison, Sara Davison Global Enterprises

United Kingdom

WHY DID I WROTE THIS BOOK?

Welcome to Make More Money from Speaking

This book represents twenty incredibly challenging and rewarding years that encompass my business and speaking career journey. It's been a culmination that has given far too many highs and lows for most people's liking, but I'm forever grateful for having done so.

My goal for this book is simple: to help you make more money speaking. My aim is to simplify the often-confusing journey so you'll experience a lot less pain, heartache, hardship, confusion, and overwhelm than *my family and I had to endure.*

My book will save you time and simplify the path so that your journey towards becoming a well-paid speaker will be as clear and seamless as possible.

In fact, I feel completely confident saying to you that after you have finished reading this book, you will transform into a better person than you were when you started this book. Being able to speak and speak effectively to any size audience at any time makes you into a different person, a brave leader if you will. They say that speaking in public is what most people fear the most, more than death. Once you finish and implement the steps in this book, you will feel more confident and wiser than when you began. But most of all you will know the secret to making money from speaking.

If you have Attention Deficit Disorder or a short attention span (like me) or you learn better and faster with videos, then go to https://www.makemoremoney-speaking.com/resources where you can watch several transformational videos with downloadable tools and resources.

I created this book for you. If you want to make more money, get a pay rise, close more clients, be seen as an icon in your industry, expand your brand or be asked to appear on TV and radio, then this book is for you.

After going through this framework myself and serving as an advisor to hundreds of clients and business associates that call me for my perspective, advice, and feedback on their encounters within this field, I am compelled to share all that I've learned.

Here's what you can expect from this book and the additional bonus video content so you get the most out of it in the shortest period of time.

First, it's interactive. I have deliberately created lots of opportunities for you to go deeper into the content and have given you personal access to free videos, resources, and other tools. Go to https://www.makemoremoney-speaking.com/resources

Second, this book is intended to help you make more money—with no BS! I have no hidden agenda. My only incentive is to share my experiences and my "version of the truth" to make sure you succeed as a well-paid speaker.

Third, it's for people who want to grow as a person, not just survive—no matter what it takes. I tackle several controversial points of view in this book, and at times it may push your belief systems. I want you to enjoy this book, but I'm not here to make you comfortable or to be your best friend. I'm interested in transformation. Transformation comes from doing something different and experiencing the results that come from taking action. In other words, you have to implement my framework to get the results – to get the money – to transform from where you are now to where you want to be. So, if you already have a preconceived notion of what you think is right or wrong in terms of making money from speaking, you might as well just close this book right now and enjoy your day.

However, if you want no BS and the simple truth from someone who has been and is still in the trenches, someone who has interviewed and talked to hundreds of speakers around the world, then I can give you this fresh perspective.

Fourth, this book isn't intended to be an award-winning book. It's designed with one thing in mind—to start a conversation with you, to give you and me a chance to get to know each other better and develop a bond. It is ultimately written to give you the tools, knowledge, and resources to master the skills of presenting so you will be well rewarded for your speaking.

Fifth, this book, although deliberately short, it is packed with step-by-step, easy-to-implement recommendations and lots of ideas. My intention is to inspire you, motivate you, encourage you, and give you clarity, focus, and knowledge, so you can deliver an engaging and profitable presentation each and every time. I'll be the first to admit that I am very opinionated. I am a person with strong ideas, but each and every one of them is backed up with a significant amount of research and results, my own success and that of my private clients.

If you like what's in this book, I'd absolutely, positively love to hear from you, get to know you better, and have you share your success story, your transformation, your picture or a video, and comment on my Facebook wall at www.facebook.com/garylafferty.

The best way to start a relationship with me is to visit the link in this book at https://www.makemoremoney-speaking.com/resources and sign up to download valuable information and to stay in touch. Please feel free to share this book with anyone you know who is in need of a transformation in his or her own personal or business life.

Sincerely,

Gary

Gary Lafferty

London, UK

P.S. I wrote and edited this book myself and with the help of a couple special people in less than two weeks. There are absolutely, positively some spelling, grammatical, and layout errors. I am also British so my Mac has defaulted to British English. If you find one, will you do me a favour and send me an email to errors@garylafferty.com. Note the page number, sentence, and mistake, and I'll fix it right away. Thank you for your help in advance. I'm all about results, which take a plan implementation and subsequent transformation.

P.P.S. If you love this book or you've found it helps you or someone you care about, will you please post a review on Amazon? Nothing would make me happier than to hear your personal transformation story and your feedback.

P.P.P.S. If you don't like this book, will you please just send me an email and tell me why? I will gladly give you your money back. Please be kind. I have a mother and two children and they all read what people say about me online and so do their friends! There's no sense in posting nasty, negative comments if you just don't like it. Just please message me and I will refund you immediately.

WHY SHOULD YOU READ THIS BOOK

Before we start, do not worry about public speaking.

Making money from speaking is easy! I know that is a very bold statement considering that most people would rather die than speak in public. The fear of public speaking, or gloss-phobia as it's known in the scientific world, is as real as night and day. But actually it is not the fear of speaking in public that is the actual underlying fear. It is actually the fear of the unknown, the fear of making a fool of yourself, and the fear of not knowing how it will go or what people will think of you.

Let's just start with this premise. Forget about public speaking for the moment. Think of it as being a passion champion—a champion for a passionate cause, a champion for your work or business, a champion of a point of view.

As a champion you may see yourself as a messenger or a spokesperson. You are someone who has an idea that you are so passionate about that you just can't wait to share your thoughts and expertise on it and about it to others.

And as a champion of your particular passion, role, or idea, speaking out and sharing is by far the easiest and quickest route to success. The very fact that most people are afraid of public speaking is exactly why there are so many opportunities to make money from it. The good news is that there is no magic to great and profitable public speaking. It's simply a system, a step-by-step system that you can use to make yourself more successful. It's an easy system to eliminate the fear so you can enjoy reaping the benefits public speaking brings and the success that comes from it.

Success means different things to different people. To some it's monetary. To others it's climbing the corporate ladder. To another group of people it means freedom from the shackles of everyday life. Whatever your idea of success is, speaking out and speaking up is the fastest way to get you what you want. If you do not learn to speak up for yourself or what you believe in you will not be rewarded. Who else can speak up for your passion more than or better than you? More than that, if you have a product or service or skill that can benefit others, by not speaking up thousands of people who would benefit from your message, won't.

****

Have you ever noticed that the same people always seem to dominate a situation or conversation? Do they seem to gain more success and recognition than others?

By speaking in front of others and sharing your point of view on a topic, idea, or passion, you move not only forward but also upward in people's view of you. You are no longer at the back of the room being ignored but front and centre where your audience is hanging on to your every word. Later in this book I will show you how to engage with any size audience and have them begging to know more about what you have to say. Being the champion of a point of view will enhance your career, build your business, and dramatically improve people's opinion of you.

Speaking successfully is merely a skill set that can be learned. Most people's fear comes from the idea of making a fool of themselves. This is mostly due to the fact that most of them when called to speak do not what to say, when to say it or who to say it to. These skills can be learned quickly and mastered over time. The steps that I teach you in this book will remove your fear of speaking in public and demystify how the most successful speakers in the world become successful.

Throughout the entire course of this book you will discover how successfully speaking in public will create an extraordinary life for you, a skill that will enable you to gain that promotion at work or new job that you have always wanted, and a method to book more business and gain more clients, to build your business by ten X. And of course, how about traveling the world and getting paid for it? I will share with you exactly how many others and I have done just that over the years. How to go from being unheard and unseen as a no one to becoming someone people want to hear from and listen to—and, in some cases, becoming recognized as an industry icon.

In the first chapter you will learn why speaking is the easiest way to gain success.

In the next chapter, you will learn how the to open your presentation and use storytelling and your own story to engage and enthral your audience.

In the third chapter, you will learn how to hone in on your own expertise and knowledge and be seen as the expert.

In chapter four, you will learn how to package your knowledge and create assets that people will want.

In the fifth chapter, you will discover how to get your audience to let you know that they want more of your knowledge by taking the next step as their desire for more grows.

Chapter six is about where to speak for the most money, what audiences pay what and where to find them.

In the seventh chapter you will learn the steps to perfect your presentation so you deliver like a pro each and every time.

In the eighth chapter, you'll learn the secrets to putting on events that produce awesome and profitable results as well as getting on other peoples stages nationally and internationally.

In the ninth and final chapter, I will show you how to put all of this together so that you can start making money, great money as a well paid speaking almost immediately. I will also give you access to some fantastic resources to help you get stared straight away.

You will no doubt know by now that some of the most successful people in your company or industry are not necessary the ones who work the hardest. Nor are they the ones who know the most. They are the ones who understand leverage. They understand and live by the rule of work smarter not harder. By becoming a champion of a topic or cause or even just a point of view and simply sharing by speaking up in front of the right audiences, they have leveraged themselves to the top.

By becoming a speaker in your field or passion, you elevate yourself. You become seen as the expert, the go-to person. As your visibility increases, so does your value to the world—and what you can charge for it.

> *'You don't get paid for the hour. You get paid for the value you bring to the hour.'*
> *Jim Rohn*

Why do you believe most people are afraid of public speaking? It's the same reason why anyone would be afraid of anything—it's because they never learned how to do it. And because they never learned to speak in public, they never did speak in public. No one in the public arena heard his or her message or point of view. They did not build their credibility. They stay in the darkness and do what others want them to do because nobody knew how great or passionate they were about what they knew.

****

System versus Framework

According to the Oxford dictionary, a system is defined as - *A set of things working together as parts of a mechanism or an interconnecting network; a complex whole.*

In other words, a system is everything you need to make something work. It is the whole thing. For example, *'fluid is pushed through the whole system of pipes to clear the blockage'* or *'The move is part of the government's plans to overhaul the criminal justice system.'*

However, a framework as defined in the dictionary is as follows - *A basic structure underlying a system, concept, or text. A plan of action designed to achieve a long-term or overall aim.*

A framework is a plan of attack to obtain a goal or accomplish an end. It consists of a starting point and a finishing point.

From what I have seen in business, the framework makes the difference, not the system.

For example, let's take a game of basketball. The system is the same no matter who plays. Take control of ball, put more balls in basket at other end, and stop other team from putting balls in your basket. That's it. That's the system. But what makes the difference in the actual results is the *framework*—the underlying plan.

Over the last decade and more I have taught thousands of people the importance and value of framework. A framework enables you to follow a set of rules and a path from A to Z. it allows you to start by taking small steps, small risks and getting more comfortable with each one. As you take each step and move closer to your goal of reaching Z, you become more confident in your abilities and your confidence in reaching your target.

You already know by now that some of the world's most successful people and leaders have all had one thing in common. They have mastered the power to communicate, the power to communicate their message to an audience no matter how large or small. Some notable examples include Abraham Lincoln, Winston Churchill, Ghandi, Mother Teresa, Billy Graham, Martin Luther King Jr, and more recently Steve Jobs.

This is why I took it upon myself to teach people how to communicate, how to speak up and be heard and how to make a difference —whether to an audience of one or to an audience of tens of thousands.

If you read through this book and follow the framework I set out for you, there is no doubt you will become successful. You may then also want to further your personal or business success by working more with my organisation or me personally. I only take private clients on and work further and deeper with those who seek transformation, not just information. Those who just want to stay in the same place are not usually a good fit for my programs or me.

The purpose of this book is to make you more successful. And by being more successful you will make more money, whether that is more salary if you are employed, more profits if you are in business or more funding or donations if you run a non-profit organisation.

Being a speaker, spokesperson or champion of a cause, topic, or industry will catapult your success. It is a fantastic way to grow as a person, expert, or leader. It is also one of the fastest ways to make a lot of money.

Table of Contents

CHAPTER 1 – UNDERSTANDING THE POWER OF SPEAKING

'I discovered a long time ago that if I helped enough people get what they wanted, I would always get what I wanted and I would never have to worry.'
Tony Robbins

Is it really possible to make a lot of money from speaking?

The answer is a resounding YES! There are several ways in which to make money from speaking. Which one you choose will depend on whether you make a four, five, six or seven figure income from your presentations. There are millions of dollars being made on any given day by speakers around the world sharing their knowledge, passion, and experiences with audiences eager to sit and listen.

There are three main ways that speakers get paid.

1. A Keynote Speaker - These get paid by the hour or by the presentation.

2. An Expert Speaker - The expert speaker gets paid by teaching their audiences on a certain topic.

3. A Platform Speaker - These speakers usually do not get paid for their presentation. Rather they speak and deliver content that the audience wants and then offers a product or service at the end of the presentation that the audience can buy if they want to learn or know more.

Over the years, many keynote speakers have realised that making a good living from just keynote presentations is practically impossible. Unless they have climbed Mount Everest, are a decorated war hero, an Olympic gold medallist or business guru, high paying keynotes will more than likely elude them.

I have taught professional speakers over the last decade my framework on how to sell a product or service from the stage to supplement or boost their income from speaking. They have gone on to offer their audiences their products, consulting or coaching services for thousands or tens of thousands of dollars. Other times it might just be selling their book for twenty bucks or so. Either way, allowing your audience to get to know you in a deeper and better way is critical if you want to make money from speaking.

I had generated millions of dollars in revenue from being a platform speaker long before I was ever offered a paid speaking opportunity. From the very beginning of my career I had gleaned salary rises and bonuses just because I spoke up about why I believed I was worth it to my bosses (my audience).

I later made even more money by showing my employees and team how to speak up and that in turn generated even more revenue for my company and me. Speaking to potential clients at trade shows and other various presentations enabled me to win and close so much more business and further commissions for my organisation. I then made even more money by selling the very company I had given birth to and nurtured.

But it did not come naturally. I had to learn, practise, and hone my skills as a speaker day after day over many years. It was a hard struggle, learning from my mistakes and sometimes, to my cost, expensive ones. There are many resources out there today that show you how to speak in public. There are clubs like Toastmasters and associations such as the National Speakers Association but none that actually teach normal people like you and me how to actually make money—good money from speaking.

That is why I created my Profitable Speaker Framework, so I could teach people all across the world how to take advantage of all the opportunities that are out there every single day.

How much money can you actually make by speaking?

As a keynote speaker, fees paid range from zero to more than thirty thousand dollars or more per presentation. However, in my experience, a majority of speakers globally will fall into the five hundred to two thousand dollars per speech bracket.

And for most, these fees come after many years of 'speaking for free - for the practice!' The five thousand dollars and above range is usually reserved only for the most prestigious and famous celebrities.

****

You don't have to reinvent the wheel or be the best at what you do to make money from your chosen topic. Like a lot of people in the self, personal and business development field, the name Tony Robbins is synonymous for filling huge arenas around the globe and presenting to millions of people each and every year. You may have heard of him. His personal development empire and personal fortune has been built upon the teachings and principles of NLP— Neuro Linguistic Programming.

Have you heard of Richard Bandler? Richard is the inventor of NLP and an expert in psychology. He has published many books on the subject. He is without doubt a true expert.

However, that being the case, why is it that Tony Robbins has amassed a huge personal fortune, gained an enormous following worldwide and is sought after by the likes of President Clinton and Oprah?

Why? Because he is the champion of NLP and personal development, that's why! He is the voice. He is the self-appointed spokesperson on that subject, while the inventor is known to only a small number of diehard specialists.

If, you have attended one of Tony's events you will have seen this process happen many times. For those of you who have not been, let me share with you how Tony conducts his presentations.

His main event is called 'UPW - Unleash the Power Within'. It has been attended by millions of people across the globe including

Oprah Winfrey. At the event, for which most have already paid five hundred dollars or more to attend, Tony shares his knowledge with the audience and shows them how they could have, for want of another term, 'a better way of life'. I must say that Tony's teachings have certainly changed my life as well as that of other friends and business colleagues over the years. But I digress. Within his presentation, he offers the audience the opportunity to work with him at a much deeper and personal level through his various additional programs.

His top program, the Platinum Partnership Program, which you have to apply for and be accepted onto, is … wait for it … sixty thousand dollars! And then there are the expenses for all the trips abroad! In a room of ten thousand people only around fifty or sixty go to the table to buy. That's only just under half of one percent of the room. However, that's additional immediate revenue of over three million dollars!

Later he will go on to offer his other programs, from Date with Destiny to Business Mastery—all starting at around five thousand dollars. Millions more dollars are made again.

But more importantly for me, how many people's lives is he able to change for the better there and then?

Can you now see how you can make a lot of money from speaking and by serving others at a very high level?

Many of the highest paid speakers in the world use the platform to build their credibility, exposure, business and, more importantly, their revenues by speaking. And you can too.

Let's just look at the maths here for just a minute. I will go into the actual figures later on in this book, sharing with you actual numbers from my own CRM system to give you a far better idea as to how much money you can make from speaking. But for now let's just use some basic numbers.

Let's say you spoke for ninety minutes to an audience of just twenty people.

At the end of the presentation you asked them to take the next step, which in this example is to purchase your consulting package or coaching program for two thousand dollars.

Only five people from the twenty enrol.

However, that's a ten-thousand-dollar pay cheque for just ninety minutes' work.

Do that twice a month and you're now making an additional two hundred and forty thousand dollars a year. That's what I call making money from speaking!

Over eighty percent of all the traditional 'professional' keynote speakers out there on the circuit are making nowhere near that.

I have included my Profitable Speakers Income Calculator in the free resources for you. Play around with the numbers. I can honestly say you will be pleasantly surprised when you see what you are really worth.

We all now live in the information and transformational age. People from all corners of this globe are seeking to find solutions to their very own issues and problems. And no matter what service or product you offer, when you learn to speak, you can reach a much wider audience that you can make an impact upon and be rewarded handsomely for it.

This is why I do what I do for a living as a speaker. This is why I wrote this book for you. The framework I will share with you in this book has allowed me to generate over fifty million dollars in revenue over the last ten years alone. It has enabled others that I have taught about it to break free and create the life and business they have truly desired when they have implemented what you are going to learn here.

This framework has been tried and tested in the trenches; it's not just theory. I have used this exact framework all across the world in over forty different countries – from Australia to America; from South Africa to Singapore – while sharing the stages with some of the world's best business leaders, sports legends and *New York Times* Best Sellers.

Over the course of this book, I will deconstruct my framework in such a way that no matter what you offer the world, be it consulting, investing, coaching, piano lessons or gardening tips, you will be able to present like a pro and make money from it.

****

Can I really do this?

Some of you may be wondering if this will work for you or work in your niche or business. Absolutely. If you have to deal with people in any way, shape or form then this framework will work. Every day there are opportunities for great speakers and champions of causes. You are one of them. A great speaker is just one person who talks on a subject that someone else finds interesting or essential. The information you give during your talk is valuable to someone.

If you work for a company then perhaps your opinion or idea on something could help another department. Perhaps by becoming a better speaker you can help someone within the organisation grow as a person.

Many people are promoted within their organisation because of their skills and experience, but skills and experience does not make them automatically great speakers. There are many opportunities within organisations, groups, and entrepreneurship to speak out and help transform lives for the good.

Like the Tony Robbins - Richard Bandler example. Just because you are seen as the best at something, does not make you the most profitable. However, being the best champion for a specific cause, does.

Feel the fear and do it anyway.

'The Only Way To Get Rid Of The Fear Of Doing Something Is To Go Out And Do It.'

'Every time you encounter something that forces you to "handle it," your self-esteem is raised considerably. You learn to trust that you will survive, no matter what happens. And in this way your fears are diminished immeasurably.'
Susan Jeffers, *Feel the Fear and Do It Anyway*

It is understandable that people feel the fear of speaking.

Jerry Seinfeld made a great joke based on a simple observation:

'I read a thing that actually says that speaking in front of a crowd is considered the number one fear of the average person. I found that amazing - number two was death!

That means to the average person, if you have to speak at a funeral, you would rather be in the casket than doing the eulogy!

The fear of public speaking is the most common fear and it prevents many people from achieving their potential. Imagine if you were comfortable speaking in public and took every opportunity presented, how would your life improve?

Overcoming the fear of public speaking brings you several advantages in your life and business.

Firstly you are seen as a leader. When you speak up, many of your audience will be thinking, *I could never do that!* You will be immediately seen as a brave leader as you are doing what most people are afraid to do.

You will increase your exposure within your network and field. Being able to speak to an audience widens your network and your message is heard by the many rather than the few. On top of that, how many people will then go on to tell all about you?

Gaining trust is another huge advantage you will achieve. Speaking in front of people can make you feel vulnerable. However, if your message is genuine and you come from a place of congruence, the audience will pick up on this and trust you even more.

Speaking in public redefines who you are. You are no longer confined to the silence at the back of the room. You have stepped up and voiced your message. And every time you do that you achieve something great. Your confidence will be boosted with each and every presentation you give.

But by far the biggest advantage you gain with speaking in public, in my opinion, is this… You beat your competition. As many of them will fear speaking in public, the very fact that you are the one who steps up to share your message puts you head and shoulders above your competition.

How to overcome the fear of public speaking?

There are many antidotes and exercises that you could do to cure to the fear of public speaking. However, in my opinion, nothing beats experience. The more you do it the better you become. Fear can't beat experience. Every step in this book and framework will help you eliminate that fear step-by-step, page-by-page.

It's a little known fact that the audience actually wants you to succeed. They secretly pray for you to do well as they know how much skill and courage it takes to get up there and speak up.

In all my years of speaking I never saw myself as a professional speaker. I always saw myself as a messenger. I love delivering a message that changes people's lives or businesses.

I am not known as a great orator. In fact, ironically, like most people, I actually don't like the sound of my own voice. People who know me will tell you that sometimes I actually feel shy and introverted. I don't think I am that funny or knowledgeable. But the reason why people seek me out to speak and why people take action when I speak is because I follow a framework that moves people. It moves them to take action. This is the same reason why people would want you to speak in front of them too, because when you implement the framework that I outline for you in this book, you, too, will move people with your story and your message.

By following the steps in this book you can copy my success and that of world's best presenters and leaders. This framework is proven, universal, and dateless. My wish for you is that you get excited at the possibilities that lie ahead for you and begin to master the art of making money from speaking.

You will begin to win people over and, as your experience grows along with your confidence, you will increasingly be able to engage with your audience and have them riveted to your every word. Remember, making money from speaking is about one thing and one thing alone—getting your audience to take the next step.

It is not about giving as much information as possible—that's teaching. Making money from speaking is about persuading people through educating them.

There have been many times when I have 'crashed and burned' and turned my audience from being super excited, to tremendously bored, because I gave away far too much information.

The more information you give someone, the less likely they are to actually use it. People have a very low retention rate. So if you overload their senses with information believing that you are improving their knowledge, you're actually wasting your time. Remember the old adage here —less is more!

Give less information but enough for them to be interested in taking the next step with you. If you give them too much one of two things will happen. They may have information overload. This means that they feel as though they have been shot at with a fire hose and don't take any action at all. Why? - Because the confused mind does not buy. The brain will seek safety in doing nothing rather than doing something and potentially making the situation worse.

The second reason is far more distressing. If you give them too much information they may feel they have gained enough knowledge to try and do whatever it is by themselves, without your help or guidance.

Imagine if you were discussing financial investing but they only retained ten percent of what you told them or only retained what they wanted to hear and proceeded to invest all their money into a project without knowing all the pitfalls; they may lose all their life savings!

This is why making money from speaking requires less information and more technique than people think.

The key to making money from speaking is to engage your audience in such a way that they reach a point of eagerness to know more about your topic, passion, or cause. You then end by telling them where they can get more.

In the next chapter, you will discover how to engage with your audience in such a way that, no matter how large or small in number the audience is, each one will feel as though you are speaking to them directly.

In order to engage with them you will have to connect with them at a level that interests them and they can associate with. Just being passionate about your topic or cause is not enough today. You must demonstrate that you understand your audience's needs and fears; show your vulnerability in such way that they feel instantly connected to you. Your role is to get them to take action for their own good. They are the heroes. Not you. You have to make them the champion of your story in such a way that they see what's in it for them. You have to connect with their emotions as well as their logic.

****

Key Takeaways:

- There are millions of dollars being made on any given day by speakers around the world sharing their knowledge, passion, and experiences with audiences eager to sit and listen.

- Being the best at something does not make you the most profitable. Being the best champion for a specific cause does.

- Many of the highest paid speakers in the world use the platform to build their credibility, exposure, business, and, more importantly, their revenues by speaking. And you can too.

- The cure to the fear of public speaking is experience. The more you do it the better you become. Fear can't beat experience.

- Making Money from Speaking is not about giving as much information as possible—that's teaching. Making money from speaking is about persuading people through educating them and getting them to take action.

Congratulations. You have begun your journey to becoming a very well paid speaker. The fact that you are reading this book signifies that you are already way ahead of your peers. I want to assure you that I am committed to guiding you along your journey to improving your life and business as you make more money by speaking.

Key Action Plan

What do you want to make as a speaker in the next twelve months? Go and download my Profitable Speaker Income Calculator and just enter what you want to make. Go have some fun and see what you're really worth as a spokesman or speaker.

Throughout this book, I refer to tools and resources that I have made available to you as free bonuses and downloads. These are my gift to you as a thank you for investing in my book. Simply register at https://www.makemoremoney-speaking.com/resources and you will gain immediate access to the resource area where you will find tools and resources to help you along your journey. The resource area will periodically be updated with new material as I make it available, so make sure you keep visiting.

Here is what you will find there:

- Income Calculator
- Slideshows
- Worksheets
- Templates
- Hand outs
- Scripts
- Videos
- And much more!

CHAPTER 2 - THE BREAKDOWN OF THE PRESENTATION

"Do the difficult things while they are easy and do the great things while they are small. A journey of a thousand miles must begin with a single step."

Lao Tzu

They say it's always easy when you know how.

Creating your presentation - be it a proposal, a business pitch, webinar or live on stage to hundreds of people, a full-blown workshop is not that difficult … assuming you know what to do!

Like everything else, when you know exactly what steps to take and in which order, the whole process becomes a lot easier.

Here's an example. Remember when you first sat in the driver's seat of a car as a new learner driver? Hopefully you embarked upon your journey with a competent and experienced driver by your side in the passenger seat and didn't just do it alone!

Now, in the UK, most people will learn to drive in a manual car – a stick shift, as it's known in the US – rather than an automatic. According to a recent survey, only eighteen percent of Americans know who to drive a stick shift, but in the UK over ninety percent of people will learn how to drive in a car with a stick shift.

For most of us Brits and Europeans, getting into the driver's seat for the very first time is an extremely nerve-wracking experience. I remember my first driving lesson. My driving instructor, whose name was Chris, pulled up to my front gates in a bright red Volkswagen Polo. I expected to jump into the passenger seat, but Chris got out of the car from the driver's side and ushered me into the 'command' seat.

I can still visualize my immediate thoughts as I buckled my seat belt and looked around the car. I had the steering wheel in front of me and placed my hands on it immediately and shuffled my hands around the wheel getting the feel of the thing. "I know what this does," I said to myself confidently. I then put one hand on the gear stick and pushed back and forth through the gears feeling very smug thinking, *'This is going to be so easy!'*

I then looked down and saw three pedals—three! *Heck, I only have two feet, what the hell am I meant to do here?* My confidence quickly changed to confusion as I now thought I didn't have enough necessary body parts to attempt this task.

After a few minutes of Chris explaining which pedal did what, he asked me to pull away in a slow, steady and controlled fashion. I revved the accelerator a bit and slowly raised my left leg to let the clutch out. The car started to move forward—I was actually 'driving a car'. I was actually driving the small red Volkswagen down my street for the very first time. What I didn't realise at the time was that I was revving the car so much people in the next town could hear me coming down the road. But I didn't care. I was actually 'driving'—yeah!

But before I managed to make fifty yards, reality came back to bite me as I abruptly stalled the car. My very first 'drive' had come to an end. I actually can't remember if I was more excited about achieving nearly fifty yards on my first attempt or embarrassed as it had come to such an abrupt end so quickly.

After restarting the car, resetting the handbrake, and selecting first gear again, we were off again into the new world of driving freedom.

Over time I went on to learn the other controls, the rules of the road, what to look out for etc. to make me a better driver.

I am sure that by no means am I the only person whose first experience of driving was so memorable. You might have even been the same. But now, most of us can jump into almost any vehicle, at any time, and just drive.

The same can be said for any new skill. The first time is always the most difficult as it is the unknown. The more we do the more we become proficient at it, and usually better.

Speaking is no different. Knowing what to say and when to say it is similar to driving, knowing when to accelerate, when to brake, when to signal etc. It's all in the practice of a proven framework. Do the first step, then the second, the third etc. The more you do something the more it becomes natural. We have gone from conscious learning to unconscious doing.

Let's take another example—learning a language.

It is estimated that over five hundred million people on this planet speak English. Yet it is not the most common language in the world. That honour goes to Mandarin.

To an English speaker, Mandarin when heard by a non-speaker sounds like a load of structured gibberish until you learn the rules behind the language. Then, over time, with practice – not perfect but practice nonetheless – the language eases itself into your experience and you become more familiar with it. And just like your native language, you become fluent.

In almost everything we know how to do we have to go through the four stages of learning. Knowing and adapting the four stages of learning allows us to grow as humans and have a growth mind-set.

The four stages are...

- Unconscious Incompetence

- Conscious Incompetence

- Conscious Competence

- Unconscious Competence

Unconscious Incompetence

This is defined as when an individual has no knowledge of the subject. We do not know or understand how something works or what is needed. In order to learn more we must recognize our incompetence in this subject and be willing to accept we don't know what we don't know.

Conscious Incompetence

This is where we understand what we do not know but we want to learn more. We are not afraid to progress further and accept that this is where most of our mistakes will be made. At this level is usually where we feel most vulnerable and the desire to quit is at its highest.

Conscious Competence

At this level of our learning we know how something works and how to do it. However, in order to complete the task we need concentration. If we take our focus off the task then mistakes will happen.

Unconscious Competence

We can now perform the task with such experience that it has become 'second nature' and can be performed with ease. Usually we can perform the task at hand whilst performing another task at the same time. We are so proficient that we can now embark upon teaching others.

****

As we progress through this book, I will take you through each stage of a presentation that I have broken down into a proven framework. Just like learning to drive a car or learning to speak another language, in order to get to the stage of Unconscious Competence in speaking you need to follow a framework that takes you through all four stages of learning.

My framework guides you through each stage so that you can create your very own presentation using the building blocks of the Profitable Speaker framework. Just like building a house, we start at the foundations and build up until we have the finished building. That being said, although we start 'building' at the foundations stage and not the landscaping, it is important that we have a set of plans – a blueprint – a map that we can follow.

Every successful presentation and every great orator follows a set blueprint, a presentation framework that builds and builds each section that engages the listener or audience and allows them to create a picture of the desired outcome.

There are three main sections to every presentation.

A. Attention

B. Body

C. Conclusion

Each section has its own framework and importance. Just as in the alphabet A comes before B and B comes before C, we must follow this path. I have seen so many speakers jump back and forth between the three sections. All that achieves is to create confusion in the audience's mind.

The human brain likes to follow a path. It likes order. When it is asked to jump from one place to another without warning, it causes confusion and switches off to preserve energy.

A confused mind does not buy.

It doesn't matter what message you are trying to convey, if you cannot get your audience's buy-in, then your message is lost.

Just like when you are watching a movie, a play or reading a book, there is a defined beginning, middle, and end—as easy as A, B, C.

A - Attention

A good, powerful, meaningful, and engaging opening is vital to the success of your presentation. Get this bit wrong and you'll lose the interest of your listener almost immediately.

Let's step into their shoes just for a moment. Your audience, being one person or a roomful of people, will almost always fall into one of two categories—wanting to be there and listen to you or having to be there and listen to you. They either made an effort to ensure they heard your message or made a sacrifice because they have to listen to you.

For example, an audience that has paid to come and hear you speak on a topic they are very passionate about or want to know more about would make an effort to hear you.

However, an employee who has be told to attend a workshop that they don't want to attend or a corporate buyer who has to make time to hear yet another run-of-the-mill salesperson spout rhetoric on how they are the best will more than likely have made a sacrifice – usually of their time – to listen.

Have you ever sat down to watch a presentation and within two minutes you've already decided you're going to be bored senseless? You grab your phone and start checking your email and social media for someone more interesting than the presenter in front of you. If within the first few minutes you have not captured your audience's attention, then usually everything that follows will fall upon deaf ears.

The first part of your presentation is crucial. This is when your audience is most critical of you. To make matters worse, this is probably when you are the most nervous.

When I first started speaking, I was well known for 'pacing'. My team knew that ten to twenty minutes before I went on stage, I would pace back and forth going over my speech in my head. They knew to stay away and let me 'deal' with my nerves in my own way. They also knew that if someone were to approach me in this vital period of self-reflection they would be doing so at their own peril.

I was like that because I thought nerves were good. I believed that being nervous before a presentation gave me the necessary adrenaline that I needed to go out there and smash it! And, in fairness, in the beginning it did work for me. That ten to twenty minutes 'pre-speech' period built up so much adrenaline and energy in me that as soon as I stepped on stage I was ready to go. And boy, did I go.

You see I was so pumped up and full of adrenaline that I used to come out and launch straight into my presentation, usually at a hundred and fifty miles an hour! I was like a racehorse cooped up in the starting blocks and as soon as the gates opened I was off!

I would take at least a couple of minutes before I would settle down to a steady pace—when my nerves had eventually calmed back down and I had relaxed into my presentation.

Unfortunately, it took me a long time to realise that my poor audience had mostly felt that they had just been spoken to at such a pace it was like taking a 'verbal' soaking from a fire hose! Well that certainly got their attention! They knew I was nervous and they had to deal with the consequences of my lack of professionalism.

There had to be a better way so I conducted years of research by watching and interviewing some of the best speakers around the world. I spent many hours and thousands of dollars in a plethora of training courses from comedians to business gurus, from politicians to professional conference speakers.

Many had the same issues I did—a huge adrenaline rush and speaking at break-neck speed. It seemed that they had all accepted that this was the norm and that every speaker would and should have nerves before they present. One by one they told me that nerves are good for you and they fuel your body and brain so they are ready to take on the 'enemy'. I couldn't help ask myself, "*Since when did my audience become the enemy?*"

The cure to this ridiculous belief did not come to me until 2008. Usain Bolt had just won the one hundred meter gold medal and was being interviewed along with the other competitors. They were all asked if they were just as nervous at the beginning of the race as they were in the starting blocks waiting for the starting gun to release them. The majority answer astounded me. Not one of them felt nervous. The reason? They all without exception knew in their own minds how they were going to run their race—which foot went where, how many paces they would run with their head down before they looked up and how hard their arms would pump to give them more momentum. No nerves. Just preparation. The lesson—not one of them would lose an ounce of the precious energy they needed to win the race on nerves.

Since that day, I have learned and mastered seeing my 'race' long before I step out on stage, I no longer have time for nerves or nervous energy. I follow my framework. The result? No more pacing. I am far more calm and relaxed. The hundreds of speakers that I have taught this to are now far more confident and are in a better state of mind before they go on stage.

When you know what to say at each stage of your presentation, you can eliminate the nerves. Using a proven framework you will have a structured opening, middle and end.

An effective opening involves five main elements:

1. Gathering Questions

2. What's in It for Me?

3. Problem and Transformation

4. Your Expert Statement

5. Your Story

Now I have seen some terrible openings in my time. I really have. From the ridiculous to the truly cringe-worthy! The opening of your presentation is known as sacred real estate. Whatever you build here on this real estate is what the audience is going to build their opinion of you on. It's their point of maximum excitement and openness. You need to meet and exceed those expectations with something just as exciting and just as open.

Before I share with you a simple but powerful way to open your presentation, let me give you a few things to stay away from.

1. 'I am so glad to be here' - What a waste of time and space. Of course you're glad to be there. Your audience expects you to be glad that you are there. What's the alternative, you hate being there?

2. 'Let me tell you what I am going to talk about'- The old marketing adage of tell 'em what you're going to tell 'em, tell 'em, and then tell 'em what you told them is just so wrong here. If you were going to speak for a whole day then maybe an agenda would be nice, but for a thirty to sixty-minute presentation it is just not necessary.

3. 'Can you hear me at the back?' - If they can't hear you then they are not going to be able to answer you anyway! And if they can, you're starting your presentation by creating a negative situation. Just assume they can hear you. They will soon tell you if they can't.

4. 'I can't hear you!' - Your audience's response and engagement is a gift not a right. If they do not respond to you, all that means is you have not given them a good enough reason to yet.

5. Finally, never apologise - Never apologise for your slides, stage, audio, room layout, or anything. You're just bringing attention to the negatives in the room before you've even started. Just get on and start with what you were going to say as if you own that spot.

The point of the open in your presentation is to gather their attention. You want to engage with as many of them as you can immediately. The best way to do this is to ask them a couple of questions that they can naturally agree with there and then.

As I want to gather the audience's attention immediately, whenever I present, I immediately ask the audience two gathering questions. I know that most of my audience will answer yes to these questions. I also get them to raise their hands to answer so everyone in the room including me can see the mass engagement and compliance in the room.

Let me give you a few examples of the questions I ask when I present.

'Raise your hand if...'

- *You would like to earn more money?*

- *You would like to be a better and more powerful speaker in the next 12 months?*

- *You would like to spend more time with your family?*

- *You would like to make more money?*

- *You would like to attract more high-paying clients?*

As you can see, these are easy and universal questions that for most people are easy to say yes to!

There is also a very important psychological reason why it is important for you to ask questions at the very beginning of your presentation. Psychologically, the person asking questions is always in control of the conversation. As you want your presentation to be accepted as a conversation, asking questions at the beginning and opening a dialogue is vital.

But also by being the one asking the questions, this puts you in control of the conversation. Then, by getting them to easily answer with generic gathering questions, you are able to take control quickly.

****

The most listened to radio station in the world.

The most listened to radio station in the world is Wii FM - What's in it For Me?

Your audience, regardless of size, will be thinking a number of things now.

- What's this got to do with me?

- Why should I listen to you?

- Why should I be interested in this?

- Why now?

Here is where you have to clearly define what you are going to talk about. But rather than tell them, you want to include them. You want to engage and captivate them further. You want to take ownership.

How do you do that? Instead of telling them what you are going to talk about, basically giving them an agenda, you want to 'let them onto the court' as it were.

Again the one who asks the questions is the one controlling the conversation and, as the presenter, you want to be the one taking control.

So it's time for more questions. But this time we want to describe some problems they may be having.

Why problems? Well, people generally are lazy. They would rather do nothing and stay with the status quo than do something, even if they know there's a better way. Unless ... unless they begin to feel some form of pain. And if you want them to do something, you need to engage them emotionally and show them the pain of being in the current situation that they are in.

After you have succeeded in getting them to see and accept the actual pain they are currently dealing with, whether they realize it or not, you should now show them the importance of an alternative way. Not necessarily your alternative, but an alternative nonetheless.

Again, you want to ask and not tell. By asking they have to answer. And with each answer they 'self-qualify' themselves.

Let me give you a couple of examples here.

- 'Perhaps you are sick and tired of having to get up every morning and repeating the exact same thing you did yesterday, only to see competitors half as talented as you grow and gain more business?'

- 'Have you ever felt that, no matter how hard you work, there always seems to be more month than there is money?

- 'Maybe it's just that you would just like to spend less time at work and more time with your family and loved ones?'

Can you see how personal these questions are? They are also quite generic. There is a reason for this.

You want your audience to not only agree with these statements but also actually feel the pain of being one of those people living in that situation.

Be careful here. Don't lay it on so thick that they switch off. We already know humans would rather ignore pain than deal with it until it's too late.

Watch the reactions of your audience carefully. Look for what's known as the 'nodding dog syndrome'. When done correctly, depending on your audience, some of them might just quietly nod their heads gently in agreement, while others might scream out, 'Hell yeah, that's me!'

Next describe three opposites to the pains you've just revealed.

- 'Now imagine a life where you are such a great client magnet that your competitors just can't figure out what you're doing to grow the way you are.'

- 'What would it be like to always have enough money every month no matter what the economic situation is?'

- 'How would you feel if one day you woke up and decided that you just wanted to take the day off to spend with your family and loved ones, and you could do so without feeling guilty or being judged?'

Can you imagine how your audience would be feeling right now? You've shown them the pain that they are tolerating and also the alternative life they could have.

****

The final part of this section is known as the bridge. You want to create a bridge of possibilities that you can show them to reach the other side.

You now want to segue between the pain that they are living or dealing with, and the better possibilities ahead. Not only that, you want to show that there are other people in the world doing exactly that and crossing their own bridge.

'Well, the good news is it doesn't have to be that way. Every single day there are people just like you finally waking up to the fact that they are no longer going to tolerate a way of life that does not serve them and at last are beginning to live their ideal lives—lives they truly deserve."

'What I am going to share with you in this presentation is how you can do the same.'

How do you think your audience will be feeling right now? What do you imagine they will be thinking?

When done correctly, you will have them on the edge of their seats eager for you to talk more and show them how to make the 'crossing' to their new, better lives.

Remember the four questions that most audiences will ask:

- What's this got to do with me?

- Why should I listen to you?

- Why should I be interested in this?

- Why now?

Even though you have opened up your presentation with broad and generic, yet also personal questions, you have now painted the pains and alternatives for your audience. Also, the four questions have also been answered. Their part of the brain that needs clarification has been satisfied all except one more important fact— why should they listen to you?

Why should I listen to you?

People in general want to understand who you are, where you came from, and why you are qualified to speak to them. You, on the other hand, want them to take some form of action – the next step – at the end of your presentation. People only tend to act upon instructions if they trust the person giving them.

If they don't trust you they won't act. And if they won't act, what was the point of your presentation?

Just as there are four levels of learning, there are three levels of creating trust. In order to get someone to trust you, they must go through these three levels.

1. Know You

2. Like You

3. Trust You

People tend to trust others that they like and they tend to like those that they know. How many times have you met someone and had an instant distrust of them or you just didn't like them, but after getting to know them a bit more you ended up not only liking them but trusting them as well?

That's the three levels in action. Like, know and trust.

As a speaker, the audience needs to get to know you and the only way they are going to be able to do that is if you open yourself up and share some personal details about yourself.

Facts TELL but stories SELL!

Here is where you have to be careful. Your audience doesn't want to know your resume. They are not interested in you at this stage of your presentation; only in why you are 'qualified' to speak to them. Case in point, when I say qualified, I am not talking about your skill level or degrees or experience.

Theodore Roosevelt once said,

'People don't care how much you know until they know how much you care.'

Yes your qualifications are important, but not as important as your story. Later on in your presentation, there will be plenty of opportunities to show off your qualifications. But at this stage of the presentation, all you want to do is build a really strong rapport with your audience.

To do this you need to show them that you are 'just like them' and that you have no special powers. You have walked in their shoes or at the very least understand them as human beings and not just as an audience.

Everyone has struggles in their life and you should show that you are no different. You must, without exception, if you want to build trust, share your story and share it with honesty.

This is one of the hardest for most speakers and does take time to master. Most speakers feel embarrassed or vulnerable so they hold back from sharing. Unfortunately, the audience can sense that you are not being totally open and are holding something back. They will not engage with you until they feel comfortable with you. Sharing your story is the quickest and most congruent way to get your listeners to know you, like you and trust you in one fell swoop.

They want to know your struggles. Your rags to riches story if you will. Your background.

When I present, depending on my audience, I will always share a story, which will include all of the following:

Who, What, Why, Where, When, and How.

Some examples of what I share are:

- Who I am

- What my mission in life /business is

- Why I do what I do

- Where I have come from

- When my life changed

- How I did it

The structure is

1. Your Expert Statement

2. Your Secret

Here is an example of my story…

I am a 2-time international bestselling author and have taught over one hundred thousand people all over the globe from America to Australia, from South Africa to Singapore, on the subject of 'How to Make a Year's Income in Just Ninety Days'.

My Profitable Speaker Framework has enabled people just like you to completely change their lives within three months and now earn two, five, and even ten times more money than they were earning before in half the time.

But it has not always been that way! What most people don't know about me is that I was brought up in a very traditional Asian household, except that my parents were divorced and my lovely but tiny five-foot-two Chinese mother had to bring up three young children by herself.

Being the eldest child, my upbringing made me more determined to do whatever I could to look after my mother and siblings… However, nothing went as planned. I barely made it through high school. I didn't get into university and I had tried and failed at twelve different careers before I found my first success…

When you openly share the struggles you had to endure, that's when your audience receives and accepts that you are 'just like them'. And if you can make it or be a success at whatever you're talking about, so can they.

By sharing your story and your struggles before you share your successes, you allow people to get to know you as a real person. Only then will they allow themselves to begin to like you and eventually trust you.

When you come to share your successes, it is important to align them with your audience's needs and wants. Always remember that the goal is to make your audience the hero, it's not your opportunity to boast about your own accomplishments. Your successes should not be random but clear and concise.

What is the result that your audience is trying to achieve? Maybe they have been struggling with a particular issue and you have overcome that exact same issue or you found another, easier or simpler way of achieving the desired result.

Some presenters I have worked with find this part quite uncomfortable. They sometimes feel that this somehow is bragging or showing off. It is not at all. Actually, when you understand that you have something that will be of benefit to your audience and that allows them to become the hero of the story, it becomes all about them and what they can achieve and not about you.

This part of the presentation is actually crucial. It shows them that there is another way. A better way. A possibility that they can achieve the same if not a better result.

The very fact that you have achieved these successes actually reinforces your right to present to them and to share your story.

At this stage of your presentation, your audience is still asking, "Why should I listen to you?" By sharing your successes you reinforce the nagging doubt they have in their minds of, *does this really work?*

You become the social proof that what you're about to present to them is more than just theory. It actually works.

My success story typically goes something like this...

'If you fast forward to today, as a speaker, I have been extremely blessed to have spoken on stages across the globe with some of the most talented business leaders and celebrities past and present.

'I am also very honoured to have been featured on many national and international media outlets including Fox and CNBC.'

It is important to finish off with a good, strong segue here, giving them a link into the next section of your presentation.

Now that you have answered the question, "Why should I listen to you?" the next stage is to actually take your audience smoothly into the next section of your presentation.

An example of a smooth segue would be,

'Over the next thirty minutes, not only will I share with you how you can achieve the exact same results I have had, if not better; I will also show you many mistakes I made along the way so that you won't have to deal with them or navigate them for yourself. Do I have your permission to show you?'

By gaining their permission to move on with a rhetorical question, it allows you to move into the next section seamlessly.

In the next chapter I will share with you the essential steps you have to take in order for the audience to see you as an expert, a person of authority. I will also show you how to package your expertise in such a way that your audience will be falling over themselves to learn more from you, even after your presentation has long finished.

Are you ready? Would it be OK to show you?

****

Key Takeaways:

- In almost everything we know how to do we have to go through the four stages of learning. Knowing and adapting the four stages of learning allows us to grow as humans and have a growth mind-set.

- Every successful presentation and every great orator follows a set blueprint, a presentation framework that builds and builds each section that engages the listener or audience and allows them to create a picture of the desired outcome.

- A confused mind does not buy.

- The first part of your presentation is crucial. This is when your audience is most critical of you. To make matters worse, this is probably when you are the most nervous.

- Psychologically, the person asking questions is always in control of the conversation.

- The most listened to radio station in the world is Wii FM! What's in it for me?

- When you know what to say at each stage of your presentation, you can eliminate the nerves. Using a proven framework you will have a structured opening, middle and end.

- The point of the open in your presentation is to gather their attention. You want to engage with as many of them as you can immediately. The best way to do this is to ask them a couple of questions that they can naturally agree with and say yes.

- When you openly share the struggles you had to endure, that's when your audience receives and accepts that you are 'just like them'.

Well done. This was a very long chapter with lots of things to take on board. The beginning of every journey tends to be the hardest until you get into your stride. You are now well on your way to making a lot of money as a highly paid speaker.

Key Action Plan

What are your keys opening questions? Go and download this chapter's worksheet to help you create your own powerful opening questions to immediately engage your audience's attention.

If you haven't already done so, make sure you register at https://www.makemoremoney-speaking.com/resources to gain immediate access to the resource area where you will find tools and resources to help you along your way. The resource area will periodically be updated with new material as I make them available, so make sure you keep visiting.

Here is what you will find there:

- Income Calculator

- Slideshows

- Worksheets

- Templates

- Handouts

- Scripts

- Videos

- And much more!

CHAPTER 3 – THE BODY OF YOUR PRESENTATION

Very narrow areas of expertise can be very productive. Develop your own profile. Develop your own niche.
Leigh Steinberg

In this section of your presentation, you will be introducing your audience to your core message. This is the body of your presentation.

Remember there are three main sections to every presentation.

A. Attention

B. Body

C. Call to Action

In the last chapter we covered the opening of your presentation. A good, strong opening will grab your audience's attention, whereas a weak one will send them and you to a social media graveyard.

****

B - Body

The body of your presentation is where you show your true expertise. This is where you show your audience that you understand who they are, what their needs are, and how to provide them.

That is not to say that you should be a 'one stop shop' and try to provide all things to all people. Definitely not! In fact, your aim is to show that you are truly an expert in a very unique and fundamental issue and that you are the go-to person in that niche.

Many speakers fall into what I call the 'Jack of all' industries. They try to show the audience how clever or knowledgeable they are about all manner of subjects. In fact, all they actually achieve is proving one or all of the following.

- You actually know far less about a particular subject than you say and are more of a generalist

- You serve no one or sector in particular and are not fussy who you work with

Or worse still...

- You tried to explain so much that you actually ended up confusing the audience

You will hear me say this over and over again, 'The Confused Mind Does Not Buy!'

If the audience can't see or feel that you are truly an expert in a particular field, you will become what is known as 'familiar' in their brain. In other words, they've heard it all before and nothing seems new. All they hear is just the usual day-to-day rhetoric that they hear every single day.

Have you ever switched off when someone is speaking to you and your brain just wandered off?

Or how about this? What was the last thing you saw on television? You could probably answer that one. But what if I asked you what was the last advertisement you saw on television? Not so easy, is it?

That's because your brain went into what I call 'boring mode'.

It's the same 'yada, yada, I've heard it all before' jargon that bombards our brains every single day. Digital marketing experts estimate that most Americans are exposed to around four to ten thousand ads each day. At some point, we start a screening process for what we engage with and start ignoring brands and advertising messages unless they're something we have a personal interest in.

Just think for a moment how incredibly complex our brains are. Our brains at any given moment can sift through billions of bits of data. For most computers, they will just freeze and potentially show the blue screen of death…you know what I mean!

However, somehow our brains find a way to organise all this information. It's called the reticular activating system.

Basically, the reticular activating system, or R.A.S. for short, is a bundle of nerve cells filtering out all unnecessary information that we receive so it can focus on getting the important stuff through.

The R.A.S. is the main reason why when you focus on learning a new word, you start hearing that same word everywhere. It's why the last time you thought about changing your car you started noticing the exact same car on the road all the time. It's not that they all suddenly appeared or everyone decided to buy the exact same car you did at the same time. They've always been there. You just never noticed them before.

Your R.A.S. automatically takes what you focus on and creates a folder or filter for it. When sifting through all the messages it receives every minute of the day, it will filter out everything that does not match the filter and only give you what you focus on. Pretty clever, don't you think?

R.A.S. also works on your beliefs and validates them. You set the parameters that the R.A.S. works to. It allows you to see the world through your beliefs as it has filtered out anything that does not match those parameters. If, for example, you believe you are going to give a bad presentation, then the chances are your brain will start believing it as true and you probably will end up giving a terrible speech, which in turn, you will end up believing it as fact. If, however, you believe that you are going to absolutely smash it out of the park, then your brain will begin to expect it and help you deliver a fantastic presentation.

Our reticular activating system can be trained. It will do what we want it to do. It will hear what we want it to hear and it will notice what we want it to notice.

This is why we can block out so much of what our eyes and ears are subjected to every day and are able to see and hear what we want to. It's our R.A.S. working at full speed in the background.

Everybody has a reticular activating system working for him or her twenty-four hours a day. Just like any given member of your audience, if what you share in your presentation does not activate or trigger their R.A.S., your message will automatically be diverted to their junk drawer.

As speakers and entrepreneurs, it is our duty to give insight and not the standard rhetoric.

How do we do this? How do we sound different? How do we break through the R.A.S. filter and get our audience to actually hear what we have to say? Surely what we have to say is rarely anything new. Probably not. Sometimes there will be a groundbreaking discovery that the world needs to hear, but in general most of what we do, say and offer is pretty similar to our competitors or peers.

The way to pierce their filter and get their R.A.S. working for us is to tap into what they see and feel is important to them. Now, although that may seem pretty obvious, I have seen and heard far too many speakers go on and on and completely miss the mark— the 'R.A.S. hotspot' if you like.

The secret is surprisingly simple. Having presented over twelve hundred presentations in over forty countries, I have developed a way to dial into the audience's R.A.S and at the same time present myself as the expert, go-to person in my niche.

I have broken it down into four steps so that you can easily do the same.

1. State three doubts, problems, myths or misconceptions that they have about your topic

2. Explain what happens if nothing is done about them

3. Share your idea or strategy to fix them

4. Give examples of, or suggest, what life would be like after

Depending on the length of time that you have for your presentation, you can repeat these four steps with a different doubts, problems, myths or misconceptions as many times as you would like. That being said, I would suggest that three issues in any given presentation regardless of time are more than plenty.

1. State the three doubts, problems, myths or misconceptions they have about your topic.

As simple as it sounds, one of the best and easiest ways to show your expert status is to point out the obvious.

What is the main problem or doubt that your audience is facing that you can firstly understand and can also solve? Is there a common myth or misconception that is widely believed that you can banish?

It doesn't matter what these issues are. Every single person on this planet deals with and tolerates a problem or believes in a myth, if not several, every single day. This is why there are so many opportunities for great speakers around the world today.

The late night infomercial industry is absolutely booming. In fact, the latest figures show that it's even gone on to eclipse the TV industry itself!

Collectively, the U.S. market for infomercial products stood at one hundred and seventy billion dollars in two thousand and nine and went on to exceed two hundred and fifty billion in two thousand and fifteen. In fact, DRTV [direct response television] is now much, much bigger than TV itself.

Why is this important?

It goes to show that people are always looking for something better, something to make their lives easier or make them feel better.

Claude C. Hopkins, one of the great advertising and marketing pioneers, once said,

'Prevention is not a popular subject, however much it should be.'

What can be derived from that famous quote is that, although prevention should outsell cures, it doesn't. People will rarely look to prevent something happening. They'd rather stick their head in the sand until it's too late and they have to do something about it ... whatever it may be.

Investor Dina Routhier said this about how important stating problems were.

'The most common thing that pegs an entrepreneur as an amateur is when they come in and immediately start talking about their amazing new technology, and forget to start the discussion with, "What is the biggest problem in the market am I trying to solve?" - If they don't start with the problem, then I know they are green.'

How many issues in your industry or niche do people have to deal with every day?

Here are some really common examples…

- Attracting new clients/business/staff

- Increasing revenues/sales/profits

- Decreasing costs/expenditure/attrition

- Managing time/staff/clients

- Saving marriages/relationships/reputations

- Improving skills/resources/processes

- Reducing accidents/conflicts/wastage

- Obtaining better health/wealth/friendships

- Online/offline/remote/onsite

- Personal/business

The list goes on and on. How about common myths and misconceptions?

Here are a few that I'm sure you've heard of…

- You're born into the life you end up with

- Entrepreneurs can only be successful if they have large funding backing them

- You can only be successful if you're first

- Entrepreneurs have to do everything themselves

- You have to take huge risks to be successful

- Entrepreneurs are never stressed out

- All I need is a million-dollar idea

- If you drop your food on the floor, it's safe to eat if you pick it up within five seconds - sorry, had to throw that one in

I'm not going to waste precious real estate here, but I'm pretty confident that, no matter what industry you are in, there will be issues and challenges that you can name immediately.

You can see that you don't need to be a jack-of-all-trades to make good money as a speaker. You can easily be a master of one or two and make a lot of money.

2. Explain what's happens if nothing is done about it.

People are inherently lazy. What I mean by that is most of us believe in the mantra, 'If it isn't broke, why fix it?'

Most people would rather tolerate something until they can't deal with it anymore than do something about it.

Usually this is because, quite simply, they believe or understand that change is more difficult that keeping with the status quo. It is safer and easier to stay and deal with it than to change it. As Darwin said…

'It is not the strongest of species that survive, nor the most intelligent; it's the one most adaptable to change.'

There is generally a lack of motivation to change. Too many people in my experience are usually so busy being busy that they believe they simply don't have the time to improve their lives or businesses.

That is where I see great speakers step in. They provide insight. They provide an alternative to the norm. They provide a plan, a plan of action that someone – provided that they are the right someone – can take to begin to improve or change their situation for the good.

As a speaker, your main role is to make a difference to your audience. To do that you must make them aware of the problem they are facing and, more importantly, what the consequences are of not taking action to improve it.

It's just like a doctor who carries out a health check on her patient. If there are absolutely no problems with her patient, the doctor can provide a clean bill of health and send her patient away with no more than a few advisory words to keep her patient as fit and healthy until her next check-up.

But in the real world very few of us are blessed with perfect health until the day we leave this beautiful green earth. Between Mother Nature and old age most of us are only allowed to grace this earth for less than a century. And as we get older, there are usually more health issues we have to deal with.

Now imagine you went for your annual check-up. On the whole, you look after yourself and generally feel in good health. However, there is this 'one thing' that's been bothering you. It's no big deal. Nothing you can't tolerate on a day-to-day basis.

As you finish up getting yourself dressed again after your examination you sit back down in front of the doctor at his desk. Your doctor looks at you and says, 'Jim, I've got good news and I've got some bad news for you.'

What would be going through your mind now? What would you be feeling?

'The good news is in general you are in relatively good shape *for your age!*' he continues.

'However, the bad news is that your what's-it-ma-call-it level is double what it should be.'

'Oh, is that all?' you reply.

The doctor then goes on to explain to you exactly why having high what's-it-ma-call-it is bad for most people. However, in your case, as your results have shown that you are double what it should be, unless you change your lifestyle immediately, in his expert opinion and experience, you will die inside nine months!

Now what would you be thinking?

He continues to explain that he has come across far too many patients over the years that have ignored this warning message and have indeed gone on to die.

'But before they died they went through six months of absolute agony. They could no longer work. The household income dried up. The family suffered financially. But worst of all the impact upon the family members that were left behind was devastating. All because they thought it was easier to do nothing than to take action!'

How would you be feeling now?

He continues by suggesting that he has a proven plan that, if started immediately and followed rigorously, could not only reduce your what's-it-ma-call-it levels but actually get rid of it completely. 'But you must act now to avoid the pain that the others experienced and had to go through.'

Now some might call this scaremongering! But is it?

Was the doctor wrong in pointing out that your levels were too high?

Was he being irresponsible by sharing his experiences of how lack of action by others had impacted them?

Would you call the doctor unprofessional because he suggested a plan that would not only decrease your levels but possibly eliminate them completely?

No. That was his job. That was his obligation as a professional in his field. That was his way of making his patient the hero of the story and not himself.

3. Share your idea or strategy to fix them.

So you have highlighted the problem or myth. You have made your audience aware of the consequences of not taking action.

Don't skip the last step. In order for them to take action at the end of your presentation you must get to 'own' the issue or problem. They must already be in a position mentally and emotionally where they are saying to themselves, and preferably to the person next to them, 'Heck, he's talking about me! How is he doing that?'

Now that you have them taking ownership of the issue and understanding the consequences of not taking action it is the time to share your idea or strategy.

It is important not to give away the ranch here. You want to compel them to take action *with you* and not by themselves. By giving away too much of the answer or cure or system at this stage, you stand the risk of them just taking that piece of advice and trying to do something by themselves.

As you have no doubt heard before, a little knowledge is a dangerous thing. By giving people too much information, you can mislead people into thinking they are more expert than they really are.

They could then go away and 'try' what they think you told them and have disastrous results. And guess whose fault it would be? Yep—yours!

Less is more.

In a ninety-minute presentation, there simply is just not enough time to explain everything to your audience or teach them in depth your whole system or solution.

In order to maintain the balance of giving the audience great value and not giving away the store, it is important that you explain that, as in all things, it's easy to do but also easy to fail if not done right.

You will serve your audience far better by focusing their hearts and minds on getting excited about the idea and taking the next step with you rather than trying to understand everything there and then. Always remember that the purpose of you speaking in front of them is to allow them to see you as the expert and for them to take action.

There are two schools of thought here.

The first way is to drip feed only partial information touching on every element. Not too much but just enough to keep the audience interested and engaged but not fully informed of anything.

The train of thought here is that, by only giving the audience a percentage of the knowledge they need to succeed, they will want more and will therefore pay to get the rest.

This is what I call the 'Skim' method.

By only giving away the skimmed version, you have piqued your audience's desire for the actual outcome. However, by only skimming the surface and not going into too much detail, the audience has to take the next step with you if they want to learn how to actually get the results.

An example would be, say, a mac and cheese dish.

In the Skim method you would tell your audience that you need all these ingredients on the list. You would then mix the ingredients together in the right order at the right time and, voila, awesome mac and cheese.

Notice, although you gave away the list of all the ingredients, you didn't actually explain how to mix the ingredients together—or in what order for that matter. You also didn't explain who long to cook it for, how to check if it's done or still cooking. Basically, you left out all the essential bits.

The other method is what I call the 'Small Wins' method.

This method is different to the Skim method in that it actually gives away the whole system ... albeit a small building block of it. This method ensures that your audience actually receives the ingredients *and* the full recipe for a small but necessary part of the finished result. A compartmentalised approached if you like.

Let's take our mac and cheese dish example again.

You would share, wholly and without exception, the ingredients, and recipe for, let's say, how to make the roux, the base of this amazingly awesome cheese sauce. Now, we all know that there are several other steps in making an awesome mac and cheese dish, but, due to time restraints, you only have the time to show them how to make the delicious mouth-watering cheese sauce and that you are the expert by explaining exactly what is needed to make that part of the dish.

You would list the other steps involved after the sauce but explain that there are further skills to master in order to achieve the final outcome.

By applying this particular method, the audience actually gets what you said they would get, in other words, the complete recipe and ingredient list to make the sauce—a small but necessary win. The audience has learnt a valuable lesson and skill set and you have given great information without giving everything away in your presentation.

Once again they have to take the next step if they want to get the whole recipe.

Which method suits you will be down to you and what you feel more comfortable with. Personally, I favour the Small Win method as the audience gets a small but complete 'recipe', rather than just a taster.

Over my many years of presenting a variety of products and services, both have worked equally well.

The key is the correct amount but with the emphasis on less is more. Too much information and the audience will feel overwhelmed and will lose interest. Too little or too sparse, and they will feel cheated and hard done by.

4.Give an example of or seed of what life would be like after.

Whenever possible, always give an example of what life looks like after the implementation of your idea or method.

You want to be able to prove that it works and that it is not just rhetorical theory. How will they feel? What would be better or easier in their lives? How much money will they have made or saved? What will they have learned or achieved?

****

Features and Benefits

They key thing here to remember is to speak in terms of the difference between the features and benefits of your product. Many presenters, speakers, and experts drop the ball at this stage.

It's not their fault. They've just spent the last however many minutes 'sharing' what they know or believe in. They've listed what's needed and how it works. They've shown what works and what doesn't.

However, where most speakers fail at this stage is that, usually, they have just been explaining in terms of features rather than benefits.

Features Tell but Benefits Sell!

It is important for me to state what I mean by selling at this point. It is getting your audience to take action, to take the next step—the step you want them to take at the end of your presentation.

If they see no benefit in taking action, they will take the easiest and safest option of doing nothing.

It has long been accepted that people do not buy products or services. They buy better versions of themselves. Versions that are healthier. That does not work as hard. Do not suffer as much. That are happier and wealthier.

As a speaker it is important for you to open Pandora's box and show your audience what's in it for them... Wii FM!

Do you remember Steve Jobs' presentation when he launched the iPod? He started by stating and emphasised its technical prowess by stating that it had an impressive and industry-beating one gig of data storage. But he found out that didn't work. All manufacturers would say that. If not then, certainly later!

So he changed tact and placed the emphasis not on the features but the benefits—one thousand songs in your pocket. That was impressive!

It is vital to understand that by *not* ending your point or presentation on benefits, you're actually doing a disservice to your audience. Give them what they want by showing them why your product, service, or message is that 'one thing' they've been searching for.

Finally, I believe it's important to say this. Be wary of putting any emphasis on 'fake benefits' for the sake of it or completely hiding away from your features, especially when appealing to a highly technical or business audience. Features matter and are an essential complement to the solution selling that gets prospects interested in the first place.

If you have examples of clients or past customers that have benefited from your product or service, or have examples of how a change in belief or direction has helped others, now is the time to share these.

According to Maslow's hierarchy of needs, after our physiological needs for food and water are met, our safety needs dominate our behaviour.

Not only do we need to feel safe in our financial, health, and personal security, we need to feel safe in our decision-making ability. Being able to show others that have placed their trust in you goes a long way to fulfilling that fundamental need for security.

****

Key Takeaways:

- The body of your presentation is where you show your true expertise. This is where you show your audience that you understand who they are, what their needs are, and how to provide them.

- Many speakers fall into what I call the 'Jack of all' industries. They try to show the audience how clever or knowledgeable they are about all manner of subjects.

- As speakers and entrepreneurs, it is our duty to give insight and not the standard rhetoric.

- You will serve your audience far better by focusing their hearts and minds on getting excited about the idea and taking the next step with you rather than trying to understand everything there and then.

- Features Tell but Benefits Sell

Wow, you're doing amazingly well. That was another big chunk of learning to take on board. You now know more than ninety percent of your peers. Keep up the good work. I am totally committed to helping you achieve your dream of making more money by speaking.

Key Action Plan

What are your features and how does your audience benefit from them? Go and download this chapter's worksheet to help you define your own uniqueness and how to get your audience to feel the desire for what you are offering.

Have you been to https://www.makemoremoney-speaking.com/resources yet? There you will be able to gain immediate access to the resource area where you will find tools and resources to help you along your way. And remember, the resource area will periodically be updated with new material as I make them available, so make sure you keep visiting.

Here is what you will find there:

- Income Calculator

- Slideshows

- Worksheets

- Templates

- Handouts

- Scripts

- Videos

- And much more!

CHAPTER 4 - PACKAGE AND MONETISE YOUR EXPERTISE

Speakers don't make the most money speaking. Entrepreneurs, who speak, make the most money!

In the previous chapters we revealed the first two sections of a powerful and engaging presentation. We discovered how to instantly gain your audience's 'Attention', the A of the framework, and then we broke down the four steps of the B stage—the 'Body'.

You know that at the end of your presentation you will call the audience to take some form of action. Whatever that call to action is you need to ensure that it is financially worthwhile for you. If you do not have a financially beneficial win for yourself or your business, effectively you have given away your time, knowledge, and expertise for free.

You want your presentation to ignite a fire of desire within your audience to take the next step with you.

Whether you are championing a cause for more donations or wanting to secure more clients and revenue, how you package your message to ensure a financial benefit is an essential factor.

In this chapter you will see how you can package your expertise and knowledge into a range of proprietary processes. We call these processes products because your expertise *is* the product of your hard work. And just as you decide how much of your time to give each client and for what investment, the products you create will be your proxy.

After every presentation or speech you always want your audience to want more—more of you, more of your knowledge, more of your solution. It is therefore necessary, and I would say essential, that you package your expertise and knowledge into a package that your audience can get hold of easily.

If you think about it, what was the point of your presentation? To educate? To change a point of view? To improve someone's life or business? Either way, chances are it'll take more than a well-structured presentation and a few minutes of 'air-time' to ensure that it sinks into your audience's mind.

According to a William Glasser Institute report, we forget eighty percent of what we learn on any given day. Eighty percent!

Have you ever been to a seminar or workshop, whether it be a motivational workshop or work based seminar of some kind? Research has shown that, no matter how impactful or interesting the information was, you would have forgotten the majority of what you heard within one to two weeks.

William Glasser Institute's report goes on to say that what the message was and how it was delivered will also define how much we retain.

The report states that we learn;

- Ten percent of what we READ

- Twenty percent of what we HEAR

- Thirty percent of what we SEE

- Fifty percent of what we SEE and HEAR

- Seventy percent of what we DISCUSSED with OTHERS

- Eighty percent of what we EXPERIENCED PERSONALLY

- NINETY-FIVE percent of what we TEACH TO SOMEONE ELSE

So if we only retain twenty percent of what we hear, then it could be argued that eighty percent of what we say as speakers falls on deaf ears!

I am a great fan of the Pareto Principle. Originally, the Pareto Principle referred to the observation that eighty percent of Italy's wealth belonged to only twenty percent of the population.

More generally, the Pareto Principle is the observation (not law) that most things in life are not distributed evenly. It can mean all of the following things:

- Twenty percent of the input creates eighty percent of the result

- Twenty percent of the workers produce eighty percent of the result

- Twenty percent of the customers create eighty percent of the revenue

- Twenty percent of the bugs cause eighty percent of the crashes

- Twenty percent of the features cause eighty percent of the usage

- And on and on…

So if you assume that only twenty percent of what you present is retained and eighty percent is forgotten, you need to help your audience remember what they've heard and turn their newly formed knowledge into something they can continue to benefit from.

Your proprietary process - your product is the ideal solution to their needs.

Phillippa Lally, a health psychology researcher at University College London, carried out several studies and concluded that...

On average, it takes more than two months before a new behaviour becomes automatic—sixty-six days to be exact. And how long it takes a new habit to form can vary widely depending on the behaviour, the person, and the circumstances. In Lally's study, it took anywhere from eighteen days to two hundred and fifty-four days for people to form a new habit.

In other words, if you want to set your expectations appropriately, the truth is it will probably take you anywhere from two months to eight months to build a new behaviour into your life—not twenty-one days.

Sixty-six days to form a new habit! All your presentation can do is open up the minds of your audience to the idea of a new concept, idea, or cause. You simply do not have enough time for them to understand and benefit from the true value of your message. They must experience it at a far deeper level in order for them to receive a true and real benefit.

If you truly want to impact the lives of your audience at a deeper level, then you must tell them how to take the next step. You will be doing your audience a disservice if you just get them all excited about your ideas but do not give them the road map for what or where they should go next.

That next step for your audience could be anything from showing them what book to buy and where to get it for more information on your topic to actually moving straight to purchasing your services in some shape or form. Where you choose to speak will also depend on which one of your products you will be promoting.

Where you start to speak and what product you start to promote with will depend on the topic, service, or idea that you are championing.

What you offer must be of greater value to your audience. It must be a logical step for your audience to take. It should follow a logical path onwards from your talk.

For example, if you addressed, say, three main issues or problems that your audience suffers with or tolerates, then the next step logically should be to show them your 'product', which will be your unique way to solve those same three issues. Chances are whatever you offer them at this stage may not be the final product that you wish to promote, but it should certainly be a step to move them forward in the right direction.

Ultimately, the best product to promote in my opinion is a long-term relationship with your audience. Building and maintaining a relationship with those who have taken the time to hear you is not only respectful to them and their time but can be beneficial to both you and them.

I wrote this book with the purpose of educating you and helping you become a more powerful and confident speaker so that you can be more successful in making more money for you or your business. I have laid out a proven roadmap in this for you to follow and the bonus material I have included at the end of book will give you a great start and enable you to immediately start making more money. However, my professional development organisation, offers you so much more. Depending on what you want to achieve and when, we offer you more in the way of several deep-dive in-depth training courses, personal on-going mentoring and even done-with-you programs that guarantee your results.

Building a long-term relationship with your audience is key. There will always be a certain percentage of every group that will want more of you immediately. They will take you up on your offer of getting more of you straight away. Your relationship with them has begun in earnest.

There will also be those who do want more of you and your expertise but just not right now. That's OK. When you present using the framework that has been outlined in this book, you will have successfully connected with them at a personal level and given them true value. You will still start a great relationship with them, just a different one.

The most important thing to take away here is the importance of beginning a long-term relationship. Many speakers are reluctant to promote anything at their presentation as they feel awkward and do not want to be seen as being pushy or salesy. By following the steps and framework laid out here, there is absolutely no need to come across with the 'hard-sell'. There's a huge difference between giving value and pushing products, which we will discuss later.

That being said, as discussed in an earlier chapter, there are several types of speakers out there in the world and how much money you make from speaking will directly depend on which type of speaker you decide to become.

There are many speakers out there who make a good living from speaking professionally. But, unfortunately, more often than not, that comes at a huge cost. As a paid speaker, you get paid to speak. So if you want to make a lot of money, you have to speak a lot. This usually means that professional speakers spend weeks away on the road away from their families and loved ones.

In fact, I know of one fantastic speaker based in South Africa. He travels the world speaking at various conferences for forty-two weeks of the year! Now, if that fits into your lifestyle then great. But, for most, being away from family and friends and being on the road living out of a suitcase for most of the year is just plain crazy. I can tell you from personal experience that waking up every morning and asking yourself, *"where am I today and what day is it?"* for many years is not congruent to a healthy and happy life ... or spouse!

The majority of professional speakers rely heavily on referral business. Hence they will travel from one conference to another hoping that the conference organiser will ask them back or there will be an audience member who is looking for a speaker for their next company year-end conference. These are the relationships they are chasing.

Now, there's nothing wrong in conducting a speaking business that way. It's just that's there's a far easier way. There is another way to find a far more responsive crowd of relationships that you can build and make more money from. And for that to happen you must approach this with your entrepreneur's hat on.

Speakers don't make the most money speaking. Entrepreneurs who speak make the most money!

As an entrepreneur, or someone who wanted to make as much money as possible, if you wanted to build long-term relationships, wouldn't it be far better and beneficial if you could build relationships with as many potential clients as possible? Of course it would.

That is why the most successful of speakers and spokespeople constantly strive to build a huge funnel. Every presentation they do and every speech they give is doing its part in placing as many people as possible into their funnel in order for them to create long-term relationships with the people in there.

Every presentation they give is the mouth or opening of the funnel. Every 'product' they offer their audience brings people closer to their business or financial goal.

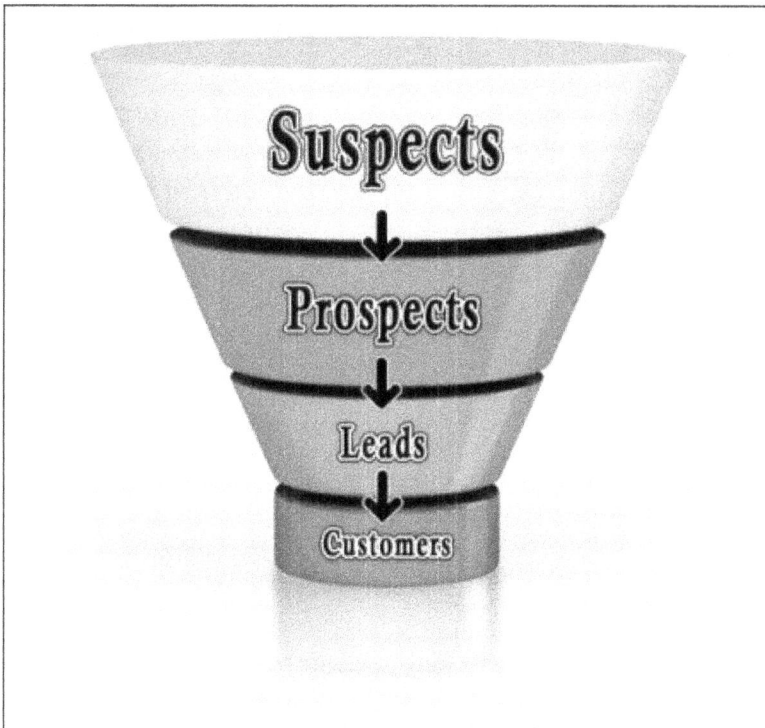

As a speaker the best product is your long-term relationship with your audience. When you present and give your audience value, education, a new point of view, or even a cause, you become the expert. You are the expert that your audience craves and their desire to learn more from you grows as they get to know you more. The further down the funnel they go the more of you, your expertise, and ideas they are exposed to.

People buy into people. You are ultimately what your audiences buy into. It doesn't matter if you're promoting a personal idea, a service that your company provides or someone else's product, if and when your audience goes into the funnel, it is because of you. You're the spokesperson, you're the speaker, and you're the expert. When you speak in front of any audience, your goal is to build up their excitement and desire to take the next step. And the next step is to get more of you, to receive more value from you. The more value you can give them the more they will benefit. If you don't have a product to offer them, and they want more of you, then what is the only thing you can give them? That's right—you, the business owner!

As this book is about making more money from speaking, I need to address the pink elephant in the room right now. If you are promoting you, then you're thinking completely upside down! You are the least profitable asset you have in your company! That's right. You're not as profitable as you think you are.

As a speaker you have to value your time. We all have only twenty-four hours a day and as an entrepreneur who speaks, our aim is to make more money per hour for our time than we can in any other way. Therefore, the reason why you are the least profitable asset is because there's only one of you. And you are very expensive.

A lot of my clients are from what I call the 'expert industry'. They are the authors, coaches, consultants, Internet marketers, entrepreneurs, network marketers, seminar leaders, and speakers. They all sell their time for money. The problem with that is because they sell their time, they can't scale.

They are the ones who provide the solutions that you and I need. They have the answers. And, unfortunately, they are often the ones who provide the answers.

Are you one of the above? Do you sell your time by the hour? By the job? By the contract? How many times in the last twelve months have you wanted to clone yourself? You see the problem with being the expert is that people expect the expert. But that is just not scalable.

What if you could get more clients, make more money, AND have more free time? Would you like that?

What if there was a way that your audience could get more of you but less of you at the same time? Intrigued?

The first step is to accept that you are the least profitable asset in your organisation. You need to charge a lot more than you do. In order to do that you need to put yourself at the thinnest part of the funnel instead of *being* the funnel.

The next step is do what you've been asking yourself to do for ages, and that is to clone yourself. And the way you do that is to clone yourself into products. The aim is to get away from hourly rates or getting paid by the job.

So what type of products can you produce and promote from the stage so that your audience gets more of you but less of you at the same time?

You have no doubt seen speakers, industry leaders and experts in their fields speak on stage and at the end of their presentation give you the opportunity to dive deeper and get more information. There are many what I call traditional products that speakers sell at the back of the room; their books, other experts' books, training material.

So what should you offer? Well, again, there are two ways to approach this. There is the 'Start Small - Grow Big' approach to the funnel or there is the 'Start Big - Stay Big' approach.

A white paper or report	$0 - $10
An eBook or published book	$10 - $20
A recorded or online program	$100 - $200
Half or full-day workshop	$500 - $1000
Bootcamp or Mastermind	$5,000 - $25,000

With the more traditional Start Small - Get Big approach that most speakers favour, the funnel or pipeline would look something similar to this:

As you can see, the Start Small - Grow Big approach usually starts with giving away something for free from the stage in exchange for some contact information such as an email address or telephone number. As your audience members get to know you better and better, over time you can introduce them and invite them to invest more time and more money to spend more time with you.

In order for you to move them through the funnel to the next level, you will need to have all your 'products' created and ready. This is time consuming but financially beneficial. As a speaker, by having a funnel, which can be mostly automated today, you can build a relationship with each and every one of your audience members who enter into your funnel.

Now, the Start Big - Stay Big approach is the opposite of the Start Small - Grow Big approach. In effect, it does what it says on the tin and starts big. This is my personal preferred method. Some of the very best speakers in the world use this approach. It eliminates the need for multiple products and offerings and aims to attract only the highest payers within the audience.

These High Ticket - High Value offerings usually start at around fifteen to twenty thousand dollars and therefore require you to have a highly skilled and polished presentation as well as proven expertise in your field.

Although I have used and continue to use both approaches in my business, I am of the opinion that if you are going to speak in front of an audience and give them great value, then you might as well get the most value from it too. I would rather speak for sixty minutes and achieve five new clients at twenty-five thousand dollars each than fifty new clients at a thousand dollars each. One hundred thousand dollars for sixty minutes! In the words of the immortal Zig Ziglar, 'And you can take that all the way to the bank!'

Aside from the obvious financial benefits, there are several other advantages of developing and promoting a High Ticket - High Value product as a speaker.

For one, as you do not have to create multiple products, you can focus and pour all of your energy and skill into creating that one great product—a product that delivers such powerful outcomes that you truly believe in and create massive value for your client. My clients have told me over the years that creating a product that people are willing to invest that much money in is truly and highly rewarding.

Your clients will be happier as they experience a superior product that serves their needs better and the amount of time and energy it takes to facilitate the product and run your business is dramatically reduced. It's a whole lot easier to run a business with fewer high value clients than lot of small offerings with loads of clients. Keeping twenty clients happy is a lot better than twenty thousand clients.

The other huge advantage is that high paying clients are usually less likely to complain. They get on with what you ask them to do and in turn get better results faster.

Delivering value is important at this level, but you also need to think about your audience's expectations. What are people *used* to paying that kind of money for?

Here are a few for you to consider:

- Personal Coaching Programs

- Home Study Courses

- Annual Membership

- Personal Training

- Ready-Made Business Models + Materials

- Business Courses

- Retreats and Trips

- Boot Camps and Seminars

People love exclusivity and expect to pay a lot of money for things where their experience is one-on-one and personal.

And, as I mentioned earlier, you are worth a lot more than you believe you are. You are the prize and they should invest heavily to get to you. Putting products between you and your audience builds anticipation and desire.

Whenever a client asks me for my number one piece of advice on how they can make more money, my answer is and always will be this—raise your prices!

How could you 'package' your expertise? Will you go Start Small - Grow Big or Start Big - Stay Big?

How could you personalise your offering to your audience more? How could you make it more exclusive, more desirable?

What product or product range could you create that will give your audience more of you but at the same time give you more time for yourself? Oh, and, of course, more money.

In the bonus download section I have included some examples used by many of the industry leaders. It is by no means an exhaustive list but it will certainly give you some great ideas.

****

Key Takeaways:

- Your proprietary process, your product, is the ideal solution to their needs.

- So if we only retain twenty percent of what we hear, then it could be argued that eighty percent of what we say as speakers falls on deaf ears!

- Your best product is your long-term relationship with your audience.

- As a speaker you have to value your time. We all have only twenty-four hours a day and as an entrepreneur who speaks, our aim is to make more money per hour for our time than we can in any other way.

- The first step is to accept that you are the least profitable asset in your organisation. You need to charge a lot more than you do. In order to do that you need to put yourself at the thinnest part of the funnel instead of *being* the funnel.

- People love exclusivity and expect to pay a lot of money for things where their experience is one-on-one and personal.

I hope you now fully understand the power of having your own unique proprietary process for whatever you do. The difference between a speaker and a well-paid speaker comes down to how well you can make yourself scalable to the market. You've done well getting to this stage, but you're not done yet. There is more greatness to come.

Key Action Plan

What is the 'product' you are going to offer your audience? Go and get this chapter's worksheet to help you with the different types of products that you can create around your expertise.

Remember to visit https://www.makemoremoney-speaking.com/resources if you haven't already done so. Gain immediate access to the resource area where you will find tools and resources to help you along your way. And remember, the resource area will periodically be updated with new material as I make them available, so make sure you keep visiting.

Here is what you will find there:

- Income Calculator

- Slideshows

- Worksheets

- Templates

- Handouts

- Scripts

- Videos

- And much more!

CHAPTER 5 - CALLING YOUR AUDIENCE TO ACTION

'You miss one hundred percent of the shots you do not take.'
Michael Scott

We are now at the most important part of your presentation—getting your audience to take action. Although this section is how you finish your presentation it should by no means be rushed. This, as you would imagine, is the C in our A, B, and C framework.

A. Attention

B. Body

C. Call to Action

Many speakers feel awkward calling people to action as they feel they are being pushy or salesy. They therefore rush through it so they can just get to the end of their 'close' as quickly and less awkwardly as possible. This is a mistake. A big one!

As I mentioned in an earlier chapter, if you rush through this part and do not give your audience a clear and easy to follow path of what to do next, you will be doing them a massive injustice.

Imagine you have just spent the last sixty minutes listening to an expert make you aware of a huge problem that is affecting your life or business that you did not know even existed. He then went on to explain all the challenges and pain you will go through if you do not take action, but he just got up and left and did not tell you where to get more help or information.

How would that make you feel? Would that maybe cause more stress? If he at least took the time to share with you what you could do to rectify this issue or where to go to get more information, at least you would have the choice of what to do next.

This section is traditionally referred to as the close. It is the natural conclusion to your presentation. Whether you have a thirty, sixty or ninety-minute presentation, I would always recommend you prepare to spend a deserving amount of time to 'close' out your talk and give your audience a clear path of what to do next.

I suggest your call to action should fill approximately one-third of your presentation. This equates to thirty minutes in a ninety-minute presentation, around twenty minutes in a sixty and ten minutes in a thirty-minute presentation.

Now, I know these numbers may seem rather long, but everything you have done and said in your presentation has led to this moment. This is a logical point to get to. If you have done your job correctly, the audience members will be eager to know how they can get more of you. All you are doing here is showing your audience how they can achieve that and pointing them in the right direction. They will make their own mind up if they want to take the path. Your role is to make that path as clear and easy as possible for them to follow.

Better the devil you know.

There are several important waypoints and hurdles that your audience will have to pass in order to get to you and your offering. These issues are usually not with you, your message, or indeed your offering. More often than not, it will be their internal psychological issues. The human brain will always search for the easiest and safest path to follow. For most people that translates to doing nothing.

You must show them that, although that is a choice they can make, and it seems safe to follow the path of doing nothing now, down the line is where the issues only get worse. You would have seeded this in your presentation earlier so all you have to do is reiterate and logically summarize the points you made earlier.

There are five steps to a successful call to action. Each step precedes the other in logical order. This order helps your audience imagine themselves following the path that you are laying ahead for them. Taking them step-by-step from where they are now to where they could be, or, even better, where they want to be. The steps are:

- Present your offer in a clear and logical way

- Describe every part of your product or service explaining to them the benefits of each part

- Add any bonuses that you are giving them and justify the value of each one

- At the end summarise all of your offers on one slide and quickly go through it in detail

- Then simply ask for the order and give them an incentive to take action immediately.

In order to lay out the path for them, where possible utilise a visual tool if possible. This could be a flip chart, a TV screen, a PowerPoint slide or at the very least pen and paper. Sometimes I will use a combination of both to really make the point clear.

Remember people only retain twenty percent of what they hear but fifty percent of what they hear and see. So by having a visual aid to assist your voice gives you a far better chance of more people taking action.

There's no such thing as a free lunch!

Everything has a price ... or should have. It doesn't matter what you are offering from your presentation, be it a 'free' consultation, a book, a consulting package or program, each and every one of those has a value. It has a monetary or result orientated value to you, and it should have a value to them. Even a 'free' consultation has a value and you must beyond all doubt believe wholeheartedly how much that is worth.

Even if you are going to be giving something away, it must have a value and you must confidently state that value. If your audience does not feel that you value your time, they will not value yours. Even if you were giving away your book that you sell for fifteen dollars, the value you should declare would be the long painstaking hours that you put into that manuscript.

Which of these examples do you feel has more value?

A. 'If you fill out the form at the back of the room, I will give you, for free, my book on saving your marriage that normally sells for fifteen dollars.'

B. 'If you go to the back of the room and fill out the pink form, you will receive my book on saving your marriage. This book took me five long years of my life and even more heartache to research and another two years locked away in my room ensuring that every single word, sentence, paragraph and chapter actually helped and made a huge difference to anyone who was reluctantly contemplating divorce but secretly in their own heart was longing for a way to save their marriage. It has helped hundreds of couple reignite their love for each other and I know it will help you too. I'm sure you'd agree if you were them you say the value of that book was priceless!'

So if you were giving away a 'free' consultation you should always state the value of that hour or session. If your hourly rate was three hundred dollars you should state that. If you were giving away a taster session, explain the value of that. Bear in mind that the value of something is relative. Just because you believe something has a value of 'x', keep in mind that your audience might not see it that way.

The best way to 'create' value in their minds is to describe it as a benefit to them.

Moving into the call to action part of your presentation should be a natural flow. This is where I have seen many speakers and spokespersons literally break into a sweat. Their whole physiology changes; their tonality raises an octave and they speed up as if the presentation is a race.

By following the framework I'm about to lay out for you, your presentation will simply 'glide' into the call to action section. Keep this thought in mind... You are offering a way to *help* your audience move from A to B, from where they are to where they want to be. The quickest, easiest, and safest way for them to achieve this is by utilizing your offering. And if you present it correctly, you will have them eager to invest and know more.

The transition from showing to offering is a lot easier for both you and them if you begin this section by asking a simple question—permission. Quite simply, the transition from the last section to this is just asking your audience's permission to reveal your offer to them.

Here is an example of something I would normally say...

'How many of you would like to have the results that these people are getting? I have created an easy to follow and even easier to implement step-by-step framework that lays out exactly what you need to do to get these results for yourself.... Would it be OK if I was to share the full system with you right now?'

That's it, just a simple question asking their permission to reveal your offer. Your audience have now asked you to show them your offer. As you both know what's coming, you can both relax and you won't feel pushy or feel salesy.

As I suggested earlier, using some form of visual aid will certainly help you keep on track as you go through your offer as well as keeping your audience engaged at each step. I tend to use a combination of slides and flip chart, but you can just use either.

Introduce your offering.

The first slide is the revealing of your 'product'. This is what your audience will receive. As you go through the rest of your product offering you will break down each component and describe the benefit and value of each so your audience can see what they are investing in should they choose to do so.

Introducing...

PS

PROFITABLE
SPEAKING MASTERY

GARY LAFFERTY

Now, you want to attract the right type of client for your product. Trying to be 'all things to all people' is a fool's game. Have your ideal client in mind and explain whom your product is right for

This Program is For...

- Coaches, Consultants, Speakers & Authors who are looking to *maximize their business income* and are looking for proven strategies that 'blow away' your clients ...and also enable you to charge more for your services
- Anyone who is just tired of *working too hard* for small results
- Anyone who is teachable and willing to follow through and *take action*

GARY LAFFERTY

Do you know whom you *don't* want to work with? Now is the ideal time to point them out too. You are actually doing them a service by pointing out that this is not for them. You don't want them enrolling or investing only to discover later that it's not a good fit for them.

This Program is NOT For...

- Anyone who is looking for a *Get Rich Quick System* and isn't committed to helping others
- Anyone who is happy with the *see how it goes* methodology towards sales and marketing
- Anyone who likes to *moan, complain* or not see things through
- Anyone who *is lazy and an excuse maker*

GARY LATTERY

What You Will Learn...

- So here is what you will get in each Module:

- Module 1: Create Your Signature Talk
- Module 2: Package Your Expertise
- Module 3: Automated Lead Machine
- Module 4: Your Authority Website
- Module 5: Industry Icon Marketing

GARY LATTERY

What You Will Learn...

- Module 6: Seminar Secrets
- Module 7: Webinar Wizardry
- Module 8: Millionaire Mindset
- Module 9: Transition Mastery
- Module 10: Profitable Partnerships

Every time you reveal something from here on, you want to immediately use a phrase similar to 'which means that...' or the word 'so...' at the very least.

By revealing what they are going to get and then saying something like, 'which means that,' or 'so you can grow...', it reminds you to describe the benefit they will receive.

Learning Objectives

- **Module 1:   Create Your Signature Talk to Grow Your Business & Your Brand**

    – We will work together to create your very own powerful presentation that gets your unique message in front of more of the *right* people, so you can grow your business, brand, and network as a respected authority, expert and an influencer in your specific field.

    – We'll take your own unique personal story, all your expertise, and your exceptional techniques and turn them into **a presentation that provides huge value to your audience and leaves them wanting more from you.**

As you go through each module, you will be showing your audience the *result* they will achieve or obtain by investing with you. Each module should take them closer to the end result just like a recipe.

Learning Objectives

- ## Module 2:   Packaging Your Expertise

    – By packaging your expertise and services you can at last escape the time for money trap so many amazing coaches and consultants are trapped in. Well now you don't have to be one of them.

    – When your offer includes distinctive leveraged elements (something that isn't reliant on 1:1 face time with you to be delivered /or that you're able to create once and use multiple times), you'll quickly free up your time – and immediately increase your revenue.

GARY LAFFERTY

In the real world, very few people in your audience actually want to know the ins and outs of your product. All they want to know is the result they will receive by taking you up on your offer.

Before you move on from each module, make sure you summarize the result or milestone that they would have obtained by completing that particular module.

Again, less is more here. Just focus on the results. What is the result? What does it look like? How will they know they got there? How will they feel after they have accomplished the task?

No one is interested in how many features they are getting, just the benefits.

Learning Objectives

- **Module 3:   Automated Lead Machine Mastery**

  – You'll discover how to create your very own automated marketing sequences that consistently bring in a flood of new leads in to your business, and convert them into high paying clients.

  – Master how to use advanced online marketing tactics to generate leads, clients and income 24 hours and day 7 days a week...even when you're sleeping or on vacation.

  GARY LAFFERTY

You are the expert on stage. You are therefore their guide. They are looking to you to guide them through the maze. They want to avoid common pitfalls and 'mines' if they were to try this by themselves so make them aware of this danger. Say things like, 'I will be holding your hand as your guide as you walk step by step through the modules...'

Learning Objectives

- **Module 4: Creating Your Authority Website**

  – *Your get the idea now...What is it AND the BENEFIT they receive*

  – *What it is and the Benefit etc....*

  – *Etc...*

  GARY LAFFERTY

Once you have broken down each module, it is now time to reveal the cost or price of your product. Be confident here. If you truly believe in your product or service *and* the value and benefits that your audience will receive by taking you up on your offer, then the price you ask should reflect that value.

Reveal the price of each module one by one by restating the *results* they would achieve from each one.

What You're Going to Get...

- Profitable Speaking Mastery System $9,997

TOTAL VALUE $9,997

What You're Going to Get...

- Profitable Speaking Mastery System $9,997
- Lifetime Access to Online Membership Site $1,997

TOTAL VALUE $11,994

Talk slowly and do not rush here. You want every word and every benefit to sink in. One of the things I look for is what I call the 'nodding dog' syndrome. Have you ever found yourself listening to someone – a colleague, a friend, or a speaker on stage – and found yourself nodding with everyone in the room? That's the nodding dog syndrome.

If you see people nodding, you have what's called 'buy in'. They are agreeing with you and taking every word you say in. They are also seeing value in your price point.

What You're Going to Get...

• Profitable Speaking Mastery System	$ 9,997
• Lifetime Access to Online Membership Site	$ 1,997
• 24 Months LIVE Hot seat Group Coaching Calls	$ 4,997
• 2 x Private 30 min Jump Start Planning Call	$ 997
• 6 x Private 60 coaching Calls – Branding, Marketing, Closing Deals and Influence	$ 4,997
• Lifetime Access to Live Facebook Forum	$ 997
• Done for you Funnel	$ 9,497

TOTAL VALUE $33,479

GARY LAFFERTY

As you reveal the total price, state it confidently…

'So, as you can see, the total value of this program is ... thirty three thousand, four hundred and seventy nine dollars.'

Preferably you want to leave those words and the slide, if that's your visual aid, just there for a moment before you proceed to the next section. A comfortable long pause if you like.

It is now time to reveal your bonuses. Your bonuses are used to 'sweeten' the offer. It is important to state here that any bonuses you offer should fall into two succinct categories:

- They must complement your product
- Must have a value of at least two to three times the total value of your product

Bonuses could include some of the following:

- Blueprints
- Action Plans
- Software
- Apps
- Checklist
- Bonus learning
- Special exclusive group membership
- Additional courses
- Consulting session
- Done-with-you products
- Done-for-you applications

As you can see, the list is endless. But each one of these will enhance their learning and, if possible, expedite their results.

Fast Acting BONUSES...

• 1 x 30 min Video Critique of your Slide deck	$ 3000
• 1 x The Perfect Profitable Presentation Slide deck Template	$ 997
• My Private Skype for Direct Coaching	$ Priceless!
• Lifetime Tickets & Access to all Future Global Events	$ Priceless!

As you list each bonus make sure that you are still explaining the reason for the bonus and what that bonus would do to help them succeed in getting the results they desire. The easier you make it for them to implement and the clearer the path you place in front of them the more likely they are to take the next step with you.

All the components of the products and bonuses have now been revealed; being able to justify the total price is essential. In the example above we have a total value of over twenty-two thousand dollars.

It is important to show your audience that the value displayed is a 'drop in the ocean' compared to the value of the result they would receive. This is called the Value versus Price Justification.

By pointing your audience's mind in the direction of what they would receive rather than what they would spend, you will be able to justify the price stated in your presentation.

You must be very clear on what they will achieve and what that would be worth to them in the long run. But it is always better to ask than to tell. In other words, rather than you pushing the idea of value on them, the best thing to do would be to ask them to justify it in their own minds. In order to help them do that you must paint a picture for them of themselves in the future.

I would typically ask them something like this:

Let me ask you something.

If all this did was to allow you to deliver one profitable presentation that netted you an additional one hundred and fifty thousand dollars in the next twelve months, would that be worth twenty-two thousand dollars?

If all this allowed you to do was give up working for someone else within twelve months and spend more time with your family and loved ones instead of working day in day out from the rest of your lives, would that be worth twenty-two thousand dollars?

If all this did was to improve your sales letters, sales videos and client presentations, which made you an additional twenty percent in profits every year, would that be worth twenty-two thousand dollars?

Can you see the pattern here? It's a simple case of asking your audience, 'If you got this result, would it be worth this?'

By asking them to see into the future, where they see themselves benefitting from the result that you have been showing them, justifying the total price becomes a lot easier.

It's time to rally the troops and stir them into action.

What You're Going to Get...

• Profitable Speaking Mastery System	$ 9,997
• Lifetime Access to Online Membership Site	$ 1,997
• 24 Months LIVE Hot seat Group Coaching Calls	$ 4,997
• 2 x Private 30 min Jump Start Planning Call	$ 997
• 6 x Private 60 coaching Calls – Branding, Marketing, Closing Deals and Influence	$ 4,997
• Lifetime Access to Live Facebook Forum	$ 997
• Done for you Funnel	$ 9,497

Bonuses:

• 1 x 30 min Video Critique of your Slide deck	$ 3000
• 1 x The Perfect Profitable Presentation Slide deck Template	$ 997
• My Private Skype for Direct Coaching	$ Priceless!
• Lifetime Tickets & Access to all Future Global Events	$ Priceless!

TOTAL VALUE $36,479 +

'Well, if you understood and appreciated any or all of the above then of course you can see why it's worth thirty-six dollars!'

You then reveal the price that you want from your products. You want to introduce some scarcity here to entice them into taking action now. It must be made very clear to them that if they take too long, then the special offer is off the table. What's more, you must stand by this too.

You can offer scarcity in a number of ways, from limiting the amount of spaces available to having a time limit of when the doors close. Some of the biggest organisations in the world use scarcity to get clients to take action. From Amazon to Expedia, from Booking.com to Uber, they all use scarcity. Uber uses surcharges to book now before the surcharge increases. Amazon and Expedia use limited availability. The important thing to note is that they all want people to take action now. Not later. Now.

What You're Going to Get...

• Profitable Speaking Mastery System	$9,997
• Lifetime Access to Online Membership Site	$1,997
• 24 Months LIVE Hot seat Group Coaching Calls	$4,997
• 2 x Private 30 min Jump Start Planning Call	$997
• 6 x Private 60 coaching Calls – Branding, Marketing, Closing Deals and Influence	$4,997
• Lifetime Access to Live Facebook Forum	$997
• Done for you Funnel	$9,497

Bonuses:

• 1 x 30 min Video Critique of your Slide deck	$3000
• 1 x The Perfect Profitable Presentation Slide deck Template	$997
• My Private Skype for Direct Coaching	$Priceless!
• Lifetime Tickets & Access to all Future Global Events	$Priceless!

TOTAL VALUE ~~$36,479~~ +

They understand through all their multi-billion-dollar research that they have carried out that once you let a prospect go away and think about it, most do not return. And you should take advantage of all those billions of dollars for your own benefit. Would you agree?

What You're Going to Get...

• Profitable Speaking Mastery System and All Support	$33,479

Bonuses:

• 1 x 30 min Video Critique of your Slide deck	$3,000
• 1 x The Perfect Profitable Presentation Slide deck Template	$997
• My Private Skype for Direct Coaching	$Priceless
• Lifetime Tickets & Access to all Future Global Events	$Priceless

TODAYS ON-SITE PRICE ONLY
$9,997

The final stage is to eliminate any doubt that might still be lingering in their minds. These silent questions will be haunting them. *Will it work? Can I do this? How much will I make? When will I personally see results?*

These are all normal questions and concerns. You want to be very confident that your product will deliver the results you said they would—all things being equal. If you deliver your product or service and they do their part whatever that may be – eat it, draw it, call it, turn up or whatever it is – then they should get results. Obviously, if they don't do their part, then of course they won't get the results.

You want to be able to show that your offering is beyond reproach so much so that you can offer a cast-iron guarantee.

The better the guarantee the more comfortable they will be taking up or investing in your offer.

My Personal Iron-Clad 100% ROI Money Back Guarantee

Try the ENTIRE THING for 12 FULL months, risk free!

Join Profitable Speaking Mastery and participate in the community, go through all the materials in the program, AND jump on the 'success calls' at the end...

After completing all of those, if you feel like you aren't on track to making 100% ROI by launching your own successful live event, I'll send you all your money back. Just make sure you gave your best efforts (by completing the items previously listed) to qualify, there's ZERO risk to you!

GARY LAITERLY

The fear here is that some people will want to take advantage of you and your guarantee. Unfortunately, that's the world we live in. People are people and that's what they do.

The good news is through my own experience I have seen that a good, strong guarantee will get you more sales and that will outweigh the people who take advantage of your guarantee.

At this point some people in the audience will see great value and will be waiting for your instructions on what they should do next. Some, however, will be thinking that they have the 'recipe' now and should just go out and try to do this by themselves.

You need to let them know that they are not alone; however, they have just made the number one biggest mistake and have just set themselves up to fail.

As an example, I would say something along these lines…

Now, before you all jump out of your seats and rush to the back to claim your space, I want to share with you the biggest mistake that some people make—and that is to go and try this themselves without any support or guidelines.

They will go on the internet, spend hours searching for the easiest and cheapest option they can without really knowing what is real and proven and what is false and downright just lies.

Worse still, they get information overload, suffer from analysis paralysis, and end up doing one of two things. Either they end up doing nothing or, heaven forbid, they take the wrong path, lose a heck of a lot of money, and end up right back where they started… Either way, what a waste of time, wouldn't you agree?

The really sad thing is that they give up and think it's either them or the industry that does not work. But they'd be wrong. They just didn't give themselves the best chance possible to succeed.

Pointing out to the room what some people are thinking reinforces the fact that you are the expert in your field because those who are thinking it will know you speak the truth and those who are not thinking it will see you what you mean because you're brought it up. Strange, isn't it?

****

Key Takeaways:

- The best way to 'create' value in their minds is to describe it as a benefit to them.

- Some of the biggest organisations in the world use scarcity to get clients to take action, from Amazon to Expedia, from Booking.com to Uber.

- The final stage is to eliminate any doubt that might still be lingering in their minds. These silent questions will be haunting them.

- A good, strong guarantee will get you more sales and that will outweigh the people who take advantage of your guarantee.

You now have the complete breakdown of a powerful money making presentation. What you now possess is the exact same framework that some of the very best speakers in the world and I use to inspire, engage and empower people to take action. Now you have the breakdown and the framework, let's now look into getting you and your message seen and heard.

****

Key Action Plan

What is the price of your product and what bonuses are your going to add to give your audience more value? Go and get this chapter's templates to help you fill in the blanks to create your 'stack'.

Go to https://www.makemoremoney-speaking.com/resources if you haven't already done so. Gain immediate access to the resource area where you will find tools and resources to help you along your way. And remember, the resource area will periodically be updated with new material as I make them available, so make sure you keep visiting.

Here is what you will find there:

- Income Calculator
- Slideshows
- Worksheets
- Templates
- Handouts
- Scripts
- Videos
- And much more!

Chapter 6 – Finding Your Audience

'What you want is the opportunity to work with an audience.
Prizes after that are just a great big bonus.'
Sir Kenneth Branagh

Every day in every town and any city there are literally thousands of speaking opportunities. There are clubs wanting speakers to speak to their members. There are also organizations looking for someone to educate their staff as well as a plethora of event planners desperately searching for a speaker to motivate delegates at their next event.

If you are new to speaking, there are plenty of places to hone your speaking skills yet still have an impact on many lives. Not only will your speaking improve, so will your network of acquaintances and contacts.

It is commonly accepted within the speaking industry that you should 'put yourself out there' by offering to speak for free at any event you can. Whereas there is an element of truth to this, I believe many up-and-coming speakers out there could actually be making money whilst coming up the ranks.

Let's look at the opportunities of where to speak and then I will share with you how to monetise each one where possible.

Local Clubs.

In every town and certainly every city there will be a variety of clubs looking for speakers to speak to their members at their meetings. These groups are very easy to speak at. They usually don't expect a highly polished presentation, so if you stumble or forget your lines as it were it's no big deal. These groups include clubs like Rotary International and other local clubs, such as the Kiwis, the Lions, and the like.

Think of local clubs in your area and you'll probably be able to find a long list of them. They tend to meet every week or month. Look for

- Local history clubs

- Gardening clubs

- Wine clubs

- Food clubs

- Women's clubs

- Parents' clubs

- Photography clubs

- Cycling clubs

- Hiking clubs

- PTSs

- Sport and athletic clubs

The list can just go on and on. From Active Moms to University Alumni, your choice can be exhausting. Just pick the ones you feel would be best suited to your topic. The biggest advantage of speaking to these is name recognition. They usually don't pay speakers and will not allow you to sell to their members. However, these are good for getting your name out there as an expert in your field as you can usually speak for thirty minutes, which is considerably more time than the standard three to four minutes that local business networking groups would give you.

A good thing to remember here is that it's not important who you speak to here, but who they know or are associated with. You never know who they are connected to or what field they work in. You could speak at a seemingly low-end club and the next thing you know you are invited to speak at someone's company event.

If you do business locally then it's important to remember that these members could be your customers. You don't have to sell here. Just let them see you are the expert and they will find you.

Charities

I like speaking at charities. Although they do not usually pay speakers, nor will they buy any books or programs, they are always looking for help in fundraising. A quick search in your local city and you will find a long list of charities that you can approach. As a speaker you can help them raise much-needed funds and at the same time make money for yourself.

This is how it works: you create a presentation that you want to give; the charity will promote your presentation to its list of donor members and charge a fee for the ticket. This could be, say, forty-seven dollars. The charity provides the room, the refreshments, and all the invitations and mailing list. You just turn up and give your presentation. You then split the door take fifty/fifty. The charity makes money and so do you. That's a win-win for both of you.

Now, you could take this a step further. In your presentation you speak about your upcoming program and that you are going to offer tickets to this group at a highly discounted price of, say, two thousand dollars. You explain that a percentage of all ticket sales will go to the charity that they support. Depending on the country, they may even get a tax credit for attending. You then donate twenty percent of takings to the charity, which they will be very grateful for.

Propose this to your list of charities and, even though you are speaking for free, you will be actually making thousands of dollars while at the same time helping a great cause.

Local Businesses and Industry Organisations

This market is huge. There are hundreds of thousands of small local businesses and business organisations in any given city. All of them require training of some kind. Many of them are happy to pay for this training. Irrespective of industry or trade, they all want to be better at something and they are always looking for that marketing or that edge that pips them past the post first or in front of their competitor.

Most small businesses tend to go for sales and marketing specialists. Management training is also a very big market. This is because small and medium-sized businesses not just large corporations need it. Local governments and departments also seek management training.

Income would be mostly derived from training fees rather than speaking fees, but it also enhances your name, brand, and reputation as the expert in your niche.

Industry organisations will usually hold monthly meetings. From auditing to waste management, there are plenty for you to choose from. At these meetings they usually look for speakers or spokespeople that can improve their members' personal development.

Educational Institutions and Adult Education Centres

Today, more and more, many educational institutions are looking to improving 'after hours' adult education to supplement their income. As this sector of the educational market has shown signs of consistent growth, these institutions look to the private sector for experts outside of their usual educational curriculum.

Much of what the market is looking to learn is not on the usual higher education/degree syllabus and these subjects are in high demand. From acupuncture to inheritance tax, due to the demand from adult education there are plenty of opportunities for you to speak.

Again, this will predominantly be in terms of teaching or training, although there are more than enough opportunities for a local professor to invite a local expert to supplement the teachings.

One of the added advantages for you as a speaker is that you can always state that you spoke at or taught at a college or university. I have spoken at the infamous LSE, the London School of Economics, on many occasions. That fact alone has opened the door to many other institutions for me.

Corporate Clients

The corporate market is one of the biggest markets for speaking opportunities. There are department events and corporate meetings as well as international conventions.

These clients will pay you for speaking in a variety of forms, from training days to workshops, and, if you impress them enough, as a keynote speaker for their annual or industry conference. They not only pay you for speaking they will also buy your products, your books, and your templates for their employees to use.

The corporate budget for training, coaching and speaking is close to ten billion dollars a year worldwide so there's quite a piece of the pie ready for the taking. Speaking at this level not only earns you good money but also builds your credibility. In my experience it is quite a closed-door industry. It's definitely who you know and who knows you. However, once you're in, you're in.

One of the largest advantages of speaking to this group is the referral business. As I mentioned earlier, once you're in and do a great job for one division, the chances are you'll be invited back to present to a different division with the same organisation. It is not uncommon for, say, a bank to invite you to speak to their client care division and then a couple weeks later invite you back to speak to their client retention division.

Getting into this market is usually one or both of two main routes. The first is who you know. If you know some corporate executives and they are happy to put you forward to their superiors, then that is a good route in. If you can make the executive look good then they'll more than likely be happy to stick their neck out and suggest you.

The other and more common route to get into the corporate market is by using speaker bureaus. The bigger the corporation and the bigger the event the higher the chances are that they will not book the speakers direct and will prefer to go through a bureau.

A speaker bureau promotes speakers to corporates for their events. That's it. That's all they do. They make their money by taking a cut of the fee that the corporate pays the speaker just like an agent would. This would be on average between fifteen and twenty-five percent.

The good news is that if you have a good topic, a good show real or video and can present well, they are more than happy to take you onto their books and promote you to their clients.

The bad news is, and unfortunately this is the reality of using speaker bureaus, you really do have to be good enough to be one of their 'favourite' speakers. In a bureau mind, a favourite speaker is one that clients keep asking for. They know the speaker is popular and they know which companies are willing to pay a fee—so they know how much they can make from that speaker.

The problem is that if your topic were the same as one of their favourites, then you would be pushed to the sidelines in favour of that speaker getting suggested first. In effect, all the good dogs go to that speaker and you get the crumbs until you can prove yourself.

Words of warning here; there are plenty of speaker bureaus out there. The last time I looked there were over three hundred and twenty in the United States alone. I would be very wary of a bureau that asked you to pay to go onto their books. They might disguise it as photos, video reels, or even your own marketing package. If they were any good at getting speakers on stage, they would make their money from their cut of speaker fees, not so-called signing on fees.

Event and Seminar Promoters

Using event and seminar promoters will make the national and international markets open up for you. Around the world there are events and seminars going on every day in nearly every conference centre you know and more. These could be industry and profession based. A quick search in Google will provide you a list from the Association of Accountants Convention to The Whale Conservation Conference. If your topic would sit well in a certain profession then there are certainly many opportunities for you to speak at these events.

The promoters of these events are constantly on the lookout for new and interesting speakers that have topics that would be of interest to their delegates. This is the bread and butter of the professional speakers industry. Competition is high here so a good history and polished presentation is essential to get invited or even accepted to speak. The amount that you could earn would depend on the size of the conference but it would range from a flat speaker's fee to a percentage of the fee they charge per delegate.

There are also events that are predominantly aimed at the general public. These events are put on to teach people how to become a plethora of things like how to become a business owner, a financial trader, how to eliminate debt, how to buy a franchise, how to invest in property etc. This market specialises in the self-improvement industry. Ultimately, you can think of it as the 'How To' industry.

As the self-improvement industry has grown dramatically, there are plenty of opportunities for you to speak to audiences into the thousands. The event organisers and promoters do not usually pay speakers but will let you sell your programs and books. They will pay for the venue hire and all the promotion to get the people through the doors and on the seats and in return ask for fifty percent of whatever you sell from the stage.

There have been many speakers who have become millionaires using promoters to get them in front of as many people as possible and split the revenue. Promoters like these operate worldwide and have enabled me to speak in front of audiences as large as five thousand people. They have also helped me speak all around the world from Denver to Dubai, Singapore to Sydney, Australia.

Make no mistake, this industry is a multi-million-dollar business and is constantly on the lookout for great speakers. Once you hone your skills and can present to a large audience there is a lot of money to be made here. If you make the promoters a lot of money, you can be assured that you will be invited back again and again.

If you had a 'product' that you sold from the stage at one of these large events at, say, three thousand dollars, you spoke to five hundred people and only sold to ten percent of the room, that's fifty people. Fifty multiplied by three is one hundred and fifty thousand dollars for a ninety-minute presentation. Even after splitting that with the promoter, you walk home with seventy-five thousand for an afternoon's work. It doesn't take you many events to make a very healthy living from speaking this way. You can see why learning to speak effectively and well is one of the easiest ways to make money from what you already know.

Running Your Own Speaking Events

One of the more lucrative ways to make money from speaking is to run your own events. There are several things to consider over and above your presentation if you were to take this route.

As this is your event, you are responsible for filling it—getting the proverbial 'bums on seats'. Getting people to agree to attend and then actually attend are two different things completely. The show-up rate varies depending on a number of factors but mostly whether you decide to charge for tickets or hold a free event. Obviously, if the event was free to attend you would have a lot more people accepting the invitation than if you charged them to turn up.

However, in my experience, the show-up rate for free events is dropping, especially in the United States. In the US, for a public seminar, it is common practice to have a show-up rate –the actual number of people who agree to come and then actually put their 'bum on the seat' – of approximately fifteen to twenty percent; in the UK and Australia approximately twenty-five percent; in South Africa the figure jumps to around fifty to sixty-five percent and in other African countries such as Kenya and Zambia anything up to eighty percent.

After you have marketed the event, you now need to be able to present a great seminar, one that will lead your audience to buy your products or services. Here lies another challenge for you as the organizer of the event. Getting bums on seats is one problem but getting quality – in other words those who have the means and need to buy whatever you're selling – is another thing completely. There is no point filling a room full of people only to find out they have no money and are all broke and all took the bus to get to you.

A particular client and good friend of mine is a financial trader and used to run his own seminars teaching members of the public how to make money from trading the financial markets. His product and methodology was proven and verified by industry leaders. He held weekly ninety-minute seminars in London and around the United Kingdom. He presented his program for two thousand pounds (just under three thousand dollars).

However, depending on where he marketed, his results would vary dramatically. One week he could have a room of twenty-five people and have five enrol into his program. Another week he'd have ninety people in the room and only one would purchase.

When it comes to running your own seminars and events, it is worth remembering than quantity and quality are two different things and can have a dramatic impact and result on your profitability. Hotels and conference rooms can be quite expensive to hire, running into hundreds of dollars a day. You need to make sure you have the right combination of show-up rate and quality to ensure your success.

That being said, if you market the right way, to the right people, who have the means and need to purchase, then this is by far one of the most profitable ways to make money as a speaker. As you gain more experience in running your own events, you can then move on to promoting other speakers and take a percentage of what they sell as well at your event.

In closing of this chapter, I wanted to address the debate of free versus fee for your event. That will depend on your topic, budget, and price of product. For example, if you offered a free public event and wanted to offer a fifteen-thousand-dollar consulting package on how to become an entrepreneur at the end of your presentation, the chances of many people being able to or wanting to invest that amount would be very slim, even though you may have a full room.

However, if you charged an entrance fee, you would reduce the amount of what I call 'tyre-kickers' but have a more dedicated number of prospects in the room. You could always discount the price of entry for those who bought on the day.

****

Key Takeaways:

- The corporate market is one of the biggest markets for speaking opportunities. There are department events and corporate meetings as well as international conventions.

- Be very wary of a bureau that asked you to pay to go on their books. They might disguise it as photos, video reels, or even your own marketing package. If they were any good at getting speakers on stage, they would make their money from their cut of speaker fees, not so-called signing on fees.

- This industry is a multi-million-dollar business and is constantly on the lookout for great speakers. Once you hone your skills and can present to a large audience there is a lot of money to be made here. If you make the promoters a lot of money, you can be assured that you will be invited back again and again.

- However, in my experience, the show-up rate for free events is dropping, especially in the United States.

- When it comes to running your own seminars and events, it is worth remembering that quantity and quality are two different things and they can have a dramatic impact and result on your profitability.

You're making it real now, making it happen. All the effort you have put into this so far is about to pay off for you. You have worked hard and earned a lot. But before you go live, let's make sure you can deliver like the real pro that you are.

Key Action Plan

Where do you want to speak? Who can you contact right now? In this chapter's worksheet you can download your Profitable Speaker's cheat sheet to help you start getting speaking leads immediately.

Have you been to https://www.makemoremoney-speaking.com/resources yet? Gain immediate access to the resource area where you will find tools and resources to help you along your way. And remember, the resource area will periodically be updated with new material as I make them available, so make sure you keep visiting.

Here is what you will find there:

- Income Calculator
- Slideshows
- Worksheets
- Templates
- Handouts
- Scripts
- Videos

And much more!

Chapter 7 – Perfecting Your Presentation

'Practice does not make perfect. Only Perfect Practice makes Perfect'
Vince Lombardi

Y ou now have your completed presentation. Before I reveal the very best way that I have found, in my experience, to get booked to speak, you have to practise. Like everything else you want to be good at, you must put the time in to practise. You must find the time. Believe me, your audience will always be able to tell someone who hasn't practised and is there just 'winging' it.

Those who don't practise would say they want to come across more natural than rehearsed. They would say that it's different every time and they do not want to come across too robotic!

Let me tell you right here and now, they couldn't be further from the truth. By not putting the time in, all it does is show you up. Here are some of the things you can spot unrehearsed speakers do. See if you recognise any of them.

- Ending too early - running out of things to say!

- Going overtime - not fitting everything in the allocated time and then rushing at the end

- Lots of errs an ums - filling time as they have lost track of where they were

- Reading every word from the PowerPoint slides - not knowing what comes next

- Crowd jeers and heckles - not being able to stay on track or engage audience

- Too many questions from the audience - lack of confidence in presentation

- Etc, etc.

Presenting to any audience without practising is a disservice to your presentation and, what's more, it's disrespectful to your audience. They are spending their time to listen to you. The least you could do is spend your time with some practice.

When you practise and practise well, there is no guarantee that you will be pitch perfect every time. However, it will dramatically reduce the following, to name just a few:

- Your nerves

- Your chances of losing track of where you are

- Your chances of getting your timing wrong

- The need for fillers

And despite those who believe 'winging' it is the way forward, practice also makes you come across and sound

- More Natural

- More Confident

- More Conversational

- More in Command

- More of an Expert

- More Authoritarian

- More Professional

There is absolutely no substitute for rehearsing and practice. Just like the top movie stars that make millions of dollars; do you think they just read the script once and 'wing-it' or do you think they practise continuously to hone their craft, as they want to give the best performance they can for their audience? Yes, you may argue that if they get it wrong they can have a retake, but studios don't hire actors and pay them millions if they keep getting it wrong and running over 'studio' time.

Think of your presentation as a performance, a performance worthy of any Broadway or West End show, because that is ultimately what it is. If you want to make money, and you want to make a lot of money from speaking, then you better make sure that your message and performance are the very best they can be. The message is what your audience wants to hear. It engages them yet keeps them on the edge of their seats wanting more. And at the end of your performance, and sometimes during your well-earned applause, they are getting off their seats to go to the back of the room with their wallets and credit cards in their hand wanting to buy more of you and what you have to offer.

This is what this book is all about, making money from speaking; creating and delivering a well-crafted and even better delivered presentation to your audience that just can't get enough of you and just wants to get more. And they vote with their wallets.

When I first started speaking, people would come up to me and pat me on the back. They would tell me how inspiring I was and what a great speaker I was. They would ask me for my business card. When I enquired as to why they would want my business card when my contact details were on the order form, they would reply, 'Oh Gary, I'm not buying today, but I will let you know. Thanks for a superb presentation.'

I quickly discovered that standing ovations and pats on the back with smiling faces waiting to shake your hand did not pay the mortgage. Imagine if I walked into the bank and instead of handing over a cheque for my mortgage, I explained to the counter clerk that I didn't make any money from my profession as a speaker, but I received lots and lots of hugs and well wishes. How long do you think it would take for my house to become the bank's house?

Ask any athlete, musician, surgeon, or lawyer. Their answers would always be the same—practice makes perfect.

I have found there are many ways to practise. But there is one very powerful way today that has made the difference to my own presentation as well as almost every one of my clients that I have mentored. But before I show you how to do it properly, let me share how I used to practise when I first started speaking.

If you were with me when I used to practise my presentations in the early nineties, you would find yourself with me in my daughter's bedroom on the top floor of my house. My daughter Yannah would be at school, and her bed, which would be against the back wall, would be all made, nice and neat with her huge collection of fluffy toys and animals all sitting there waiting on her bed for her to return home from school.

Well, these were my perfect practising partners. I would line up all her toys against the back wall on her bed. I would then get my portable flip chart paper and pens ready, fire up my laptop with my presentation on it, and start the stopwatch.

I would present to my proxy live audience. I would take the time to look into each and every one of their eyes as if they were real. If I stumbled delivering my lines, I would just stop, recompose myself, and start again.

I would practice in sections, point-by-point, rather than going through the whole presentation for ninety minutes straight. And I would practise until I knew my slides back to front and inside out without looking at them. The only time I would look at my slides was when I moved to a new one—something I still do to this day.

A quick point here; you have no doubt heard of death by PowerPoint. How many times have you sat in an audience and watched as the speaker painstakingly reread every word from the slide? Awful, isn't it? Again that just shows complete lack of preparation and practice.

The slides should be there to guide you as a speaker, to act as waypoints so not only do you know where you are but also that you are on track. For the audience, less is more. The less words you can have on our slides the better—preferably a picture. They say a picture tells a thousand words and I wholeheartedly agree. A great mid-way slide would be a good quality image with three or four bullet points maximum.

If no image is used then still only keep to the minimum bullet points and verbalise the rest. As an example, if were to take one of my slides I used in the previous chapter, instead of looking like this:

Learning Objectives

- **Module 3:   Automated Lead Machine Mastery**

  – You'll discover how to create your very own automated marketing sequences that consistently bring in a flood of new leads in to your business, and convert them into high paying clients.

  – Master how to use advanced online marketing tactics to generate leads, clients and income 24 hours and day 7 days a week...even when you're sleeping or on vacation.

It could look like this:

Learning Objectives

- **Module 3:   Automated Lead Machine Mastery**

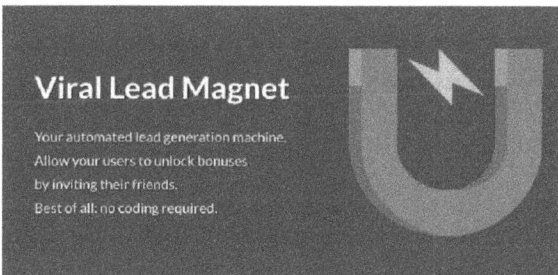

* image from www.producthunt.com

The fewer words you use on your slides the more your audience will focus on you. That will improve audience engagement and will also improve your eye interaction with them too.

The more you practise your presentation the less you will have to rely on the slides. When you don't have to rely on the slides, you will come across far more natural and convincing all at the same time. And your audience will love you for it.

So, what is my number one way to practise? A powerful way to rehearse that almost any one of you could use immediately and can do anywhere…

Use your mobile phone to record yourself speaking—that's it. Wherever you are, just pull out your mobile phone, switch it to video and record yourself and then watch it back. Now, to begin with, if you are anything like me, and like most people I have come across, watching yourself on video is not pleasant to start with. It doesn't look like you, sound like you or even seem like it could be you. But it is. It's the 'you' that the audience sees not the 'you' that you see in the bathroom mirror every day.

If using video is too much for you to handle in the beginning, the very least you should do is record yourself speaking into the phone on audio. Most phones today have a recording app or functionality on them.

I suggest using the video recording functionality to all my clients as soon as they can, as it will do tremendous things to their body stance and language. We are all mostly oblivious to the body language that we give off when we are presenting unless we are made aware of it; from walking too much around the stage to leaning on one side too often.

Practice makes perfect.

****

Key Takeaways:

- Think of your presentation as a performance, a performance worthy of any Broadway or West End show, because that is ultimately what it is.

- I quickly discovered that standing ovations and pats on the back with smiling faces waiting to shake my hand did not pay the mortgage.

- The slides should be there to guide you as a speaker, to act as waypoints so not only do you know where you are but also that you are on track.

- The fewer words you use on your slides the more your audience will focus on you. That will improve audience engagement and will also improve your eye interaction with them too.

- Watching yourself on video is not pleasant to start with. It doesn't look like you, sound like you or even seem like it could be you. But it is. It's the 'you' that the audience sees not the 'you' that you see in the bathroom mirror every day.

How did you your practice go? Did you feel odd watching yourself on video? Don't worry. It's perfectly normal. The more you do anything the easier things will become.

Are you ready to go out there and make some money? Then let's explore what you should be doing to fill your diary full of potential speaking engagements. Now go out there and start making money from speaking.

Remember, visit https://www.makemoremoney-speaking.com/resources. Gain immediate access to the resource area where you will find tools and resources to help you along your way. And remember, the resource area will periodically be updated with new material as I make them available, so make sure you keep visiting.

Here is what you will find there:

- Income Calculator
- Slideshows
- Worksheets
- Templates
- Handouts
- Scripts
- Videos

And much more!

Chapter 8 - Getting Booked on Gigs

'If you have to rely on yourself, you try harder, and when you try harder, you feel bigger.'
Margo MacDonald

In this chapter I will be showing you how to fill your calendar with lead-generating speaking engagements. Lead generation for any company and enterprise is key. And if you have chosen to use speaking as one of those generation tools, then this chapter is where I will show you what you can be doing and should be doing to get those speaking engagements.

It doesn't matter how good your presentation is or how many hours you've practised, if you can't get in front of a real audience you are not going to generate leads or money. And that is what this book has been all about, Making Money from Speaking.

There are basically two types of money making, lead-generating presentation events you can do. The first is to speak at someone else's event. The second is to create your own event. Doing both can produce some fantastic and profitable results.

Getting booked or bookings has more to do with your mind-set than anything else. This is the thing that's makes the difference. If you have nowhere to speak then you can go and make a difference to the world.

In these days of modern technology, internet, social media and online advertising, in my opinion, one fantastic tool has not only been overlooked but has almost completely been retired to the proverbial storage cupboard—and that is the humble telephone.

We all carry a mobile 'phone' around with us today. It seems as though it is permanently attached to us. It's in our hand, in our handbags, in our cars—it even goes to bed with us. Without it, we practically feel naked. It used to be our watches. If we left the house without our watch we would feel uncomfortable all day. However, if someone was to ask us the time now, we would be more comfortable and likely to pick up our phones instead and look at the screen!

Although we call it our mobile 'phone' it really is a mobile 'device'. According to recent research, we pick up our phones every twelve minutes. That's eighty times a day! It wouldn't surprise me now if you have a big urge to pick up your phone now or at least know where it is.

So although we pick up phones around eighty times a day, how many calls do we actually make?

Today's technology certainly helps and assists in maintaining a constant stream of leads for a speaking business, but to get started, there is no better tool, in my opinion, than the telephone.

Three years ago, I was asked by one of my global clients to train their staff on how to use the telephone to follow up after each and every seminar that they ran. I was commissioned to write the script for them and train it into their team.

Now, bear in mind that this team had never been to the seminar, had never met the clients they were calling and were not the speaker. They were employed purely to follow up after the speaker had presented at the seminar.

Up until this point in time, my client believed that if the clients did not buy at the seminar, they would never buy and a telephone call would be a waste of time and money. And I agreed with them.

But, like any tool, if you don't know how to use it, then the tool is practically useless. However, if you not only know how to use it but also put it in the hands of a trained professional, it becomes the best tool in the world. Imagine a blunt knife in the hands of an amateur cook compared to the *same* knife but sharpened in the hands of a master chef! Same tool - different results! Now you know what I mean.

So back to my client. The year before he paid me to come in, create a script, and train his staff, his team produced approximately twenty-five thousand dollars in that year. After six months of implementing what I taught them and using the telephone as a tool, they produced an average of twenty-five thousand dollars per month! They went from fifty thousand dollars a year to *six hundred thousand dollars* a year just by using the phone efficiently.

If you are just starting out, then speaking at someone else's event or premises is how I suggest you begin rather than running your own events. By leveraging others you will not have the initial expense of marketing and room hire, which can run into hundreds if not thousands of dollars. You can start local and build from there. Another huge advantage is that you can build up a bank of happy testimonials, which you can keep until you are ready to market you own events.

The methodology is to contact as many suitable companies, associations, and groups in your town or city as you can that you feel you can bring value to. In any given town or city you will be able to find more potential speaking opportunities than you can imagine. You then want to pick up the phone and call them and ask to speak. Don't worry about what to say as I have included a sample script that you can adapt and use in the bonus download section.

As with most things in business, what can't be measured cannot be managed, and therefore knowing your numbers when it comes to the telephone not only gives you a good idea of how well it works but also keeps you on track towards your goal.

Let's crunch some numbers now to see how this works. I will use figures that I have experienced in my own business as well as those gained from my clients.

Let's say your goal was to have eight speaking engagements per month. That's two a week. That's eight opportunities where you could speak in front of an audience that understood your product offering and had a need for it. That's definitely doable by anyone.

From the recording of numbers that I have made over the years, I can tell you that it takes on average one full hour of being on the phone to get one speaking gig. In other words, if you sit and dial for one full hour, you should walk away with one speaking engagement.

Now, there is difference between what we call a dial and a call. A dial is literally that—a dial. You picked up the phone and you dialled a number. A call is an actual call that you had with a decision maker.

Many times when you call, or dial, you will reach the gatekeeper, receptionist, answer phone or indeed there will be no answer. We don't count those as calls, just dials as you didn't manage to have an actual conversation and ask for the gig with the decision maker. And these will be recycled into your next day's calls until you get to speak to the actual person who can actually say yes and book you.

Now, here's a mind-set thing for you to remember. Selling someone else or something else is always easier than selling you! Selling yourself for most people is somehow harder as you may feel that you are bragging or making yourself out to be someone you are not. And that's perfectly normal and natural.

The way to deal with that and get over this 'I'm bragging' mentality is this. Don't book yourself. 'What? Gary, what do you mean don't book yourself? I thought that's what I was meant to be doing?'

No. You are not booking yourself. You are on the phone booking the *presentation*. The presentation is where the value is to the audience. Not you. You are merely the messenger—the messenger of a very important message, but the messenger nonetheless.

If you remember, your presentation was built around three important myths, misconceptions, or problems. In your presentation, you bring these up and show your audience how to deal with them, thus solving an issue they had. Then and only then do you offer the audience a way of getting to learn more.

When you are talking to the decision makers, you're not trying to book you but offering the organizer effectively some free training for their staff or club members where they will get tremendous value.

This is by far the best way to deal with this 'me' syndrome. You have to find a way to separate yourself from your teaching. It's just like you telling your best friends about how great the last restaurant you visited was. You can go on and on about how great the food was, the atmosphere, the staff, the music, the valet, and whatever else. It will be a lot easier if you 'brag' about your program and what it does for others and how they would feel if they took the program, rather than you as a person.

When you pitch the program as an entity rather than you as a person, you will find this transition a lot easier.

A few words of warning here. Firstly do not cheat and fall into the email trap thinking that would be easier. Pick up the phone. On the face of it, emails are easier and quicker to do. But in the long run, when you measure against success rates and efficiency, email is just a complete waste of time. More importantly it's a waste of *your* time.

Think about it from the organiser's point of view. You want to speak in person to their group but can't speak in person to them. Your words on email will never have the impact they have in person. Add that to the fact that printed words can be misconstrued, as they have no emotion attached to them. They can't convey the power of you and the power of your message.

When you call, you want to convey the value that your presentation will give the audience. If they would book you to speak, they can be assured that their members or audience would learn this skill and leave with that skill and therefore will be able to do this and achieve that, etc.

The other mistake people make is to palm this work off to someone else. We live in a virtual world now. There is always someone, somewhere on the planet that will be happy to get on the phone and try to book you places to speak at for the right price.

However, I have found that they lack one simple but powerful superpower. And that is you. Your energy, your passion, your understanding of your topic. Your empathy for your audience. Your desire to help others.

When you make the call yourself, you can adapt quicker, answer questions easier and more in depth. You build more confidence in the organiser. They have heard you personally and felt your tonality. You have managed to move him or her in such an emotional way that no telemarketer or virtual assistant can ever do.

There will come a time when you are so busy that you will engage the help of others to book your speaking gigs, as I do. But I just love getting on the phone and talking my way into my own gig. I know the value I give when I speak and the value they will receive from my presentation and my program, should they decide to invest further. But I will make ensure that I give value on the phone to the organizer and continue to give value at the presentation as if my reputation depends on it—because it does.

So when you get on the phone you need to know three things. What is the topic of your presentation? You then want to be clear on the title, a title that will engage people and pique their interest rather than turn them off. The third thing is what the audience will learn and be able to take away with them.

Here are a few examples:

Topic - Weight Loss

Title - The three foods you should be eating that you're not already

Takeaways -

One - What you should be eating

Two - Why you should be eating it

Three -Where to find it

****

Topic - Financial Investing

Title - The biggest mistakes most brokers are making and how to spot if yours is doing it to you

Takeaways -

One - What they keep missing

Two - Why you're losing money every year if you do nothing

Three -How to fix it

****

Topic - Real Estate

Title - Why paying off your mortgage early actually leaves you poor in retirement

Takeaways -

One - The number one thing you must not do

Two - How to build cash for your future

Three -Why now is the right time?

Get all this down on paper. What is it that our audience wants to hear? What do they suffer with and how can you solve it? Write out several versions and see what compels you the most.

Then go and ask other people for their thoughts. Is this something they would listen to? Is it something that would make them say, 'Hell yeah, I'd love to hear that'? Do some validation exercises with your friends and family.

However, be aware that finds and family can be the worst critics. It's not that they can be nasty, but they tend to be too nice. Let them know that you want good, old-fashioned feedback and don't hold the horses.

You will now want to create what's known as a one-sheet. This is what it says on the tin and effectively describes you on one sheet of paper. This is what organisers will want to see.

A speaker one-sheet is your writing advert of you as a person, your speaking topics, and the benefits of your presentation to the audience. It's one of the most powerful assets in your marketing toolbox that gets you in front of decision makers charged with finding engaging, relevant speakers for their event. Your job is to convince them that you are the one they should hire.

Your speaker one-sheet should answer the questions that your event organizer has before they book a speaker. These would include:

- What is your area of expertise?

- Who have you spoken to and given presentations to?

- What are the benefits that your presentation brings

    o To the leaders of an organisation?

    o For the participants in the room?

- What have you done that makes you an expert?

- Which groups have you worked with before?

- What feedback have your presentations received in the past?

- How can you be reached for more information?

- The essential elements on a one-sheet are:

A Recent Headshot

The first thing organizers want to see is your face—a headshot. If you can, use a professional, high-resolution headshot. If not then use a decent camera to take a professional picture—modern 'mobile devices' now have excellent cameras built in.

Your Name and Tagline

Create a tagline that you want to be known for, e.g.

Helen Jones – Blending executive coaching with modern Human Resources.

Your Bio

This is just a couple of paragraphs to give the organizer an idea of your experience and expertise. Use benefit statements to connect with your audience and assure them that you're in it to make a difference in their lives. Show your personality and how you are different from the other speakers out there. Include any awards or accolades to prove your place as an expert. Finally, let the reader know why you are the person to deliver this presentation.

Your Speaking Topics

List up to three speaking topics that you cover and include brief descriptions of each one. Use attention-grabbing titles by highlighting the benefits to the target audience. Keep this description brief but also engaging. The reason you want three is so that you can rotate them depending on who you are speaking to and how many times you get invited back.

Your History

Show where you've spoken before. If you're new to the speaking industry, list where you have worked before. Use company logos or list the organizations putting the largest or most prestigious ones first.

Testimonials

Without doubt, the most important part of a speaker one-sheet is your testimonial section. Testimonials are the absolute social proof that you can do what you say you can do and also that you are good at it.

They help the event organiser see your value. They want to do a good job so they are looking for as much help and assurance as possible that you are the right person to solve their problem. Good testimonials help them see the end result—a happy and grateful audience, satisfied boss, potentially repeat customers or whatever their ultimate desire might be.

Your Contact Information

Make it easy for them to contact you! Give many ways that you can be contacted and include links to your website and social media channels. Ensure you use calls to action like, 'Book (your name) Now!' or 'Contact (your name) Today' to get a quick response.

****

What it boils down to is this. The event organiser wants one thing and that's peace of mind. They want to know that people are going to have a good time; they are going to be educated and not sold to for sixty minutes. They need to be assured that you have something of value to share with their audience. They don't want a prima donna who's demanding and hard to work with. Basically they want to have an easy life.

In order for you to make this profitable let's crunch some more numbers. No doubt at these presentations you would offer great value, serve your audience at the highest level and give them the answer to solve the three problems or issues your presentation brought up.

Let's, for example, say that you had a presentation that showed local car dealerships three methods of selling one more vehicle per month. The dealership would benefit as well as the sales executives. The sales manager got you in to speak at their dealership as part of their weekly sales meeting. You now have practically guaranteed attendance.

In your presentation, you shared your three ways to sell one more vehicle each month and offered them to attend your two-day 'Double Your Sales' event that you are holding in six weeks' time at a discounted ticket rate of two hundred and fifty dollars each.

Let's say that the dealership had ten sales executives and they each learned how to sell only one more vehicle each per month. The dealership has just discovered how to make an extra one hundred and twenty sales per year—for free! How much is that worth to them financially? At approximately two thousand dollars profit per vehicle time one hundred and twenty, that's almost an extra quarter of a million dollars per year.

As your presentation has already delivered great value, chances are the sales manager will be keen to send some of his sales executives to your two-day event.

Let's say he sends four of them, keeping six in the showroom. Four tickets at two hundred and fifty are one thousand dollars for a sixty-minute presentation.

The numbers are looking good here, but you haven't finished yet. You are doing eight presentations per month. All things being equal, that's eight thousand dollars in your bank for one month of speaking. Not bad at all for eight hours work, wouldn't you agree?

But I've saved the best for last. At your two-day event you have thirty to fifty people, all who have paid two hundred and fifty dollars to attend from the two months' worth of preview presentations that you have given. You give two fantastic days of value and specific learning, showing each attendee how they can potentially earn twice or five times their earnings per year by making more sales more easily.

You then offer to mentor a few of them in your exclusive 12-month mentoring program at ten thousand dollars each. Of the fifty attendees, only seven take you up on your offer—the other forty-two decline. That's an additional seventy thousand dollars in income for you.

Can you see how the numbers keep adding up?

Finally, you will repeat this cycle maybe just six times per year.

Six two-day events per year make you seventy-five thousand dollars.

Seven from each event upgrades to your mentoring package. That's an additional four hundred and twenty thousand dollars.

That's just shy of a half-a-million-dollar income. And you still have the goodwill of everyone else that you spoke to that didn't take you up on your mentoring program.

****

Key Takeaways:

- If you are just starting out, then speaking at someone else's event or premises is how I suggest you begin rather than running your own events.

- When you are talking to the decision makers, you're not trying to book you but effectively offering the organizer some free training for their staff or club members where they will get tremendous value.

- You need to know three things. What is the topic of your presentation? You then want to be clear on the title, a title that will engage people and pique their interest rather than turn them off. The third thing is what the audience will learn and be able to takeaway with them.

- A speaker one-sheet is your writing advert of you as a person, your speaking topics and the benefits of your presentation to the audience. It's one of the most powerful assets in your marketing toolbox.

- What it boils down to is this. The event organiser wants one thing and that's peace of mind. They want to know that people are going to have a good time.

Your nearly at the end but also just at the beginning. Did you work out how much money you could make? How much make will be directly related to how much value you bring to your event organiser and their audience.

Key Action Plan

What is it that your want the event organiser to know about you and how your talk will benefit their audience? Go and download this chapter's bio sheet template to help you create your speakers one sheet.

Remember, at https://www.makemoremoney-speaking.com/resources you can gain immediate access to the resource area where you will find tools and resources to help you along your way. And remember, the resource area will periodically be updated with new material as I make them available, so make sure you keep visiting.

Here is what you will find there:

- Income Calculator

- Slideshows

- Worksheets

- Templates

- Handouts

- Scripts

- Videos

And much more!

CHAPTER 9 - PUTTING THIS ALL TOGETHER

'Be the change you want to see in the world.'
Mahatma Gandhi

I'm going to go MAD!

I am on a personal mission to help one hundred thousand entrepreneurs make one million dollars each from speaking. I believe that every business owner and entrepreneur has a message to share with the world as well as a powerful and motivating presentation to come out in order to serve others at a much higher level, to go and make a difference—To Go MAD!

Unfortunately, the biggest challenge I face is that most speakers and experts do not know what their message is or how to structure it in such a way that it engages and motivates people to take action for the better of themselves.

Imagine if you had a complete presentation that was dialed down to the tiniest detail that you could use anytime online or offline.

What would it be like if you had such an irresistible offer that it called your prospects to stand up and take action immediately?

How would you feel if you knew that, every time you delivered your presentation, you not only helped and served others at a tremendously high level but it also enabled you to generate an outstanding income year after year that not only increased your wealth by 5X, 10X or even 20X but dramatically improved your and your family's happiness?

Getting a mentor will give you the necessary roadmap to expedite your success. You have come so far along this journey by reaching the end of this book. And although you have reached the end, it is also the beginning of your journey.

Whether you choose me as your mentor or someone else, make sure you get a good one. Someone who does not just spout rhetoric, but someone who has not only been in the actual trenches, but is still there, hustling everyday, applying his or her tradecraft.

When choosing your mentor to accompany you along your path to financial gain by making more money from speaking, make sure you ask the following questions from them.

- Are they getting results?

- Are their *clients* getting results?

- Do they have all three necessary components for success – Systems, Accountability and Mindset Mentoring?

- Has their system been working for a long time and still works today?

- Does it work for a wide variety of experts?

- Do they provide world-class support?

Getting the right mentor to work alongside you is vital if you want to minimize your mistakes and maximize your chances of success in speaking – or any field for that matter!

A great mentor will give you great ideas for you personally and ensure you act upon them. They will put you together with a powerful group of people along the same path – kindred spirits if you like.

Everyone should have a mentor. They will bring you new ideas, accountability and real world battle trenches advice.

They will provide you the shortest, fastest and safest route to your desired outcome.

Our role as experts, spokespeople and speakers is to go out into the world and make a difference but also to guide the people of the world to better themselves. Whether that be personally or as businesses, we could all be better.

At life's most drilled down level, most people do not want to be trained. They want to gain results. They want to be led. And they want to be entertained.

That is why most people do not take action. They do not want to be taught. If anything, in my experience, they actually want to be Info-tained Ⓡ.

When you learn how to effectively deliver value, education, and information in an entertaining way, you, too, will be able to go MAD and help change the lives of people all around the world.

To find out how the most successful global entrepreneurs have discovered how to share their message with the many rather than the few and have managed to continue to go MAD each and everyday, reach out to me at letsgomad@garylafferty.com and lets see how you can Go Make A Difference too.

ABOUT THE AUTHOR

I was born and bred in England and schooled in Hong Kong before moving back to the United Kingdom for my higher education. After completing my formal learning I started my career as a graduate accountant for the Nestlé Corporation in London. I chose to go into accountancy as my preferred profession after failing to achieve my dream of going to med school. Since I was 7 years old, all I had wanted to do was to open my own medical practice and start working for myself instead of anyone else. So, as becoming a doctor was off the cards, I had to choose another profession that would give me the option of working for myself whilst also serving others quickly. Accountancy it was!

Unfortunately, after eighteen months, both my superiors and I realized that number crunching and me were never going to be great bedfellows. In 1987, I was fortunate enough to be taken on by another 'Fortune 500' company and became their 2nd non-graduate to be awarded a position in their field sales department. And that was the start of everything I do now.

Since then I have gone on to start, grow and sell many businesses, in many industries, not only for me but also for clients around the world.

Although I am a speaker, author, and advisor, I am no longer just one of these. The best title I can give myself is an Expert's Mentor.

I speak around 90 to 100 times a year and have given over 1450 seminars and workshops over the past 15 years. Many of these speaking engagements are self-promoted events in various industry niches as well as the traditional speaking opportunities.

I consult and advise with entrepreneurs from several areas of businesses globally as well as working with some of the largest personal and business training organizations in the world. My expertise includes selling the intangible, leadership, and scalable entrepreneurism and professional presentation skills.

I create and market specific business-building products, especially for the service profession industry. In addition to having written four other books including *Average to Expert*, *Make Money Whilst You Sleep*, *The Procrastination Handbook* and *Financial Trading for Beginners*, I collaborate and co-author with a small but personally chosen group of joint venture partners to continuously bring more value-based business solutions to market.

I run my own highly successful business advisory business and I also mentor other speakers, consultants, coaches, authors, and trainers. I work with them to maximize their income and gain more time back by creating their own value-based books and products. My work helps entrepreneurs and CEOs boost their chances of becoming the Go-to Expert Authority in their Niche.

Facebook:www.facebook.com:garylafferty

Twitter:www.twitter.com/TheGaryLafferty

Instagram:www.instagram.com/garylafferty

LinkedIn:www.linkedin.com/in/garylafferty

Amazon Author Page

www.amazon.com/author/garylafferty

HIRE GARY TO SPEAK AT YOUR EVENT!

Book Gary Lafferty as your Keynote Speaker and You're Guaranteed to Make Your Event Highly Entertaining and Unforgettable!

For over two decades, Gary Lafferty has been educating, entertaining and helping entrepreneurs, authors, experts, speakers, consultants, and coaches build and grow their businesses.

Gary Lafferty is a 2 time #1 International Bestselling Author, World Class Speaker, Expert Strategist, and Wealth Authority. He is the creator of The Business Blueprint, the ACE Business Process, and the Average to EXPERT Marketing System. He is the CEO of Bee Free Limited, a long international personal achievement training company. His products and programs simplify the process that coaches, consultants, authors, experts, and service providers follow to become the go-to person in their industry. He has taught, mentored, and helped over 100,000 people across 6 continents. His businesses and methods have produced over $50 million in revenue in professional services and courses over the last 10 years.

His unique style inspires, empowers, and entertains audiences while giving them the tools and strategies they need and want to get seen and heard and to build and grow successful, sustainable brands and businesses.

For more info, visit

www.garylafferty.com/book-gary-to-speak

ONE LAST THING...

If you enjoyed this book or found it useful I'd be very grateful if you'd post a short review on Amazon. Your support really does make a difference and I read all the reviews personally so I can get your feedback and make this book even better.

If you'd like to leave a review then all you need to do is click the review link on this book's page on Amazon.

Thanks again for your support.

Gary

www.ingramcontent.com/pod-product-compliance
Lightning Source LLC
Chambersburg PA
CBHW060610200326
41521CB00007B/724